Building Blocks for Teaching Preschoolers with Special Needs

Building Blocks for Teaching Preschoolers with Special Needs

by

Susan R. Sandall, Ph.D.
University of Washington, Seattle

Ilene S. Schwartz, Ph.D.
University of Washington, Seattle

with

Gail E. Joseph, Ph.D.
Head Start Bureau, Washington, D.C.

Hsin-Ying Chou, Ed.D.
University of Washington, Seattle

Eva M. Horn, Ph.D.
University of Kansas, Lawrence

Joan Lieber, Ph.D.
University of Maryland, College Park

Samuel L. Odom, Ph.D.
Indiana University, Bloomington

Ruth Wolery, Ph.D.
Peabody College of Vanderbilt University
Nashville, Tennessee

·P·A·U·L·H·
BROOKES
PUBLISHING Co.®

Baltimore • London • Toronto • Sydney

Paul H. Brookes Publishing Co.
Post Office Box 10624
Baltimore, Maryland 21285-0624

www.brookespublishing.com

Typeset by Auburn Associates, Inc., Baltimore, Maryland.
Manufactured in the United States of America by
Versa Press, East Peoria, Illinois.

All vignettes in this book are composites. Any similarity to actual individuals or
circumstances is coincidental, and no implications should be inferred.

Building Blocks for Teaching Preschoolers with Special Needs is based on research conducted
through the Early Childhood Research Institute on Inclusion (ECRII) supported by Grant
#HO242K4004 from the U.S. Department of Education, Office of Special Education
Programs. No official endorsement by the federal government should be inferred.

Library of Congress Cataloging-in-Publication Data

Sandall, Susan Rebecka.
    Building blocks for teaching preschoolers with special needs / by Susan R. Sandall and
Ilene S. Schwartz with Gail E. Joseph . . . [et al.].
        p.   cm.
    Includes bibliographical references (p.   ) and index.
    ISBN 1-55766-576-1
    1. Children with disabilities—Education (Preschool)—United States.   2. Children with
social disabilities—Education (Preschool)—United States.   3. Inclusive education—United
States.   4. Individualized education programs—United States.   I. Schwartz, Ilene S.
II. Title.

LC4019.2 S26   2002
371.9´046—dc21

                                                              2002016455

British Library Cataloguing in Publication data are available from the British Library.

Contents

Contents

About the Authors

Susan R. Sandall, Ph.D., Experimental Education Unit, Box 357925, University of Washington, Seattle, Washington 98195

Dr. Sandall is Assistant Professor at the University of Washington in special education with a specialization in early intervention and early childhood special education (EI/ECSE). She has directed personnel preparation projects, developed curriculum materials for all age groups, and published materials on instructional strategies to facilitate optimal outcomes for young children with disabilities. Dr. Sandall is a board member of the Division for Early Childhood (DEC), Council for Exceptional Children, and an investigator on DEC's research project to synthesize EI/ECSE research practices and translate them to recommended field practices. She is also co-editor of DEC's *Young Exceptional Children* monograph series and co-editor of *DEC Recommended Practices in Early Intervention/Early Childhood Special Education* (with Mary McLean and Barbara J. Smith, Sopris West, 2000).

Ilene S. Schwartz, Ph.D., Experimental Education Unit, Box 357925, University of Washington, Seattle, Washington 98195

Dr. Schwartz is Professor at the University of Washington in the area of special education. Dr. Schwartz has an extensive background working with young children with special needs, specifically with young children with autism and other disabilities. Dr. Schwartz is the faculty advisor for the inclusive preschool and kindergarten programs at the Experimental Education Unit at the University of Washington, where she maintains an active line of research and personnel preparation activities. Dr. Schwartz is Principal Investigator of several projects, including a model demonstration project to develop school-based services for young children with autism, a research project to assess the differential effectiveness of preschool programs for young children with autism, and a personnel preparation program for early childhood education teachers who work with children with severe disabilities in inclusive settings. Dr. Schwartz has published numerous chapters and articles about early childhood education and social validity. She serves on the editorial review boards of the *Journal of Early Intervention* and *Topics in Early Childhood Special Education.*

Gail E. Joseph, Ph.D., Head Start Bureau, Administration for Children and Families, 370 L'Enfant Promenade, SW, Washington, D.C. 20447

Dr. Joseph is Mental Health Specialist at the Head Start Bureau in Washington, D.C. She completed her doctorate at the University of Washington and was Head Teacher in an inclusive Head Start classroom in the Experimental Education Unit. Dr. Joseph's research and practice focus on the social and emotional development of young, high-risk children and mental health interventions for children and families. She is co-author of the *DEC Recommended Practices Program Assessment* (with Mary Louise Hemmeter, Barbara J. Smith, and Susan R. Sandall, Sopris West, 2001).

Hsin-Ying Chou, Ed.D., Experimental Education Unit, Box 357925, University of Washington, Seattle, Washington 98195

Dr. Chou served as Research Assistant for the Early Childhood Research Institute on Inclusion (ECRII) at the University of Washington. She has worked with young children with special needs in Taiwan and the United States. Her professional interests include parent–professional relationships and decision making. She received her doctorate in education from the University of Washington in 2001.

Eva M. Horn, Ph.D., 1122 West Campus Drive, University of Kansas, Lawrence, Kansas 66045

Dr. Horn is Associate Professor of Early Childhood Education at the University of Kansas. Dr. Horn focuses on the development of effective instructional approaches for infants and young children with developmental delays and disabilities. Her research examines how these effective strategies can be implemented within the context of ongoing routines and activities in inclusive environments. Dr. Horn is the editor of the journal *Young Exceptional Children.*

Joan Lieber, Ph.D., Benjamin Building, University of Maryland, College Park, Maryland 20742

Dr. Lieber is Professor of Special Education in the College of Education at the University of Maryland. Her research interests include inclusion and teachers' beliefs and practices. She has 8 years of public school teaching experience. Dr. Lieber co-directs an early childhood special education model demonstration project that includes young children with disabilities in community-based programs.

Samuel L. Odom, Ph.D., 3234 W.W. Wright Education Building, 201 North Rose Avenue, Indiana University, Bloomington, Indiana 47405

Dr. Odom is Otting Professor of Special Education at Indiana University. During his career, Dr. Odom has been a preschool special education and elementary resource room teacher, a student-teaching supervisor, a program coordinator, a teacher educator, and a researcher. In 1999, Dr. Odom received the Research in Special Education Award from the Special Education Research special interest group of the American Educational Research Association (AERA). In 2001, he received the DEC Service to the Field Award. Also, he has served on the National Academy of Sciences Committee on Educational Interventions for Young Children with Autism. His research addresses issues related to the inclusion of young children with disabilities in general early childhood education settings and intervention to promote the peer-related social competence of young children with autism.

Ruth Wolery, Ph.D., 2201 West End Avenue, Peabody College of Education, Vanderbilt University, Nashville, Tennessee 37203

Dr. Wolery is Assistant Professor of the Practice of Special Education at Peabody College and Director of the Susan Gray School for Children. Prior to joining the Early Childhood Research Institute on Inclusion (ECRII) team, she spent years working in the public school system. Her current teaching and research interests focus on delivering high-quality services to young children with disabilities in inclusive preschool programs.

Foreword

Since 1985, as inclusive preschool programs have become more common, our field has spent a great deal of time talking about how to design classroom environments that are developmentally appropriate for all children. We have focused on developing effective classroom schedules, designing learning centers, implementing creative activities that build on children's interests, and creating classrooms that represent caring communities. This work has been critical for ensuring that early childhood education programs provide high-quality environments for all children. During this same period of time, however, there has been a great deal of concern about the extent to which instruction occurs in early childhood education classrooms. (The term *instruction* refers here to the carefully planned use of environmental arrangements and teaching strategies to promote individualized outcomes for children, particularly those with disabilities and other special needs.)

Teachers have identified a number of reasons for this limited amount of instruction. Some feel that it is someone else's responsibility (e.g., the special education consultant, the speech-language therapist) to provide instruction on children's individualized education program (IEP) objectives, while others report that they embed instruction whenever possible, given the time constraints associated with having as many as 40 children across two sessions each day. My experiences during the last several years—preparing teachers; providing training and technical assistance to teachers in child care settings, Head Start, and public preschool programs; and conducting research on embedded approaches to instruction—have led me to conclude that the most compelling explanation for the lack of instruction in inclusive preschool classrooms is that it is a complex process that requires careful planning and implementation. This complexity is addressed in Chapter 2, "The Building Blocks Model":

The model is guided by the goals of successful inclusion and improved outcomes for young children with disabilities and other special needs in community-based early childhood classrooms. Using this model, teachers can help all of their students participate, learn, and thrive in their preschool classroom.

To accomplish this, teachers must match an individual child's goals and objectives with appropriate teaching methods and materials, decide what amount of help or assistance is needed by the child, provide this assistance, and determine whether the assistance was helpful. (p. 9)

Furthermore, they have to do this in the context of meeting the needs of perhaps 20 other children.

The authors stress the importance of a high-quality early childhood education environment and the need for collaboration among professionals and families. The process of implementing instruction is further complicated by the need for knowledge about effective classroom management. Given the breadth and depth of knowledge that is needed to implement instruction in the context of a high-quality early childhood education environment, one can better understand why instruction does not occur more frequently. The authors' understanding of the challenges associated with implementing effective instruction in inclusive preschool settings is based on years of experience with teaching young children, preparing teachers to work with young children, and conducting research on teaching young children. *Building Blocks for Teaching Preschoolers with Special Needs* reflects this experience as well as the authors' commitment to information that is useful to those who work directly with young children and their families. One of the greatest challenges in our field is bridging the gap between research and practice. I believe that the authors of this book have done this quite effectively.

Building Blocks for Teaching Preschoolers with Special Needs is the most comprehensive book available about providing instruction in early childhood classrooms. It is rare to find a book that combines all of the necessary information about instruction in one text. It acknowledges and addresses the complexity of providing instruction in inclusive classrooms by clearly describing the different levels of instruction that are needed when working with children with a range of abilities and disabilities. By doing this, the authors have been proactive in addressing a common concern among teachers that the information is not relevant for their specific context or the children with whom they work. Furthermore, it provides information and tools on planning, implementing, and evaluating instruction. It provides information and guidance on issues that often are barriers to effective instruction, such as classroom management and adaptations for children with a range of special needs. In summary, it addresses all of the relevant components of instruction in a format that will be useful to teachers. It provides both a framework for instruction and the information necessary for understanding how to implement it.

Many in our field have discussed the benefits of and barriers to inclusion and what it means to include, in a meaningful way, children with disabilities and other special needs in community-based programs. This debate has focused both on the rights of children to be included and on the supports and services that are necessary for inclusion to be successful. Although I believe that the right to inclusion has become more universally accepted, at least for the early childhood years, I suspect that we are still years away from completely understanding how to include children with a range of special needs successfully and meaningfully in community-based programs.

Building Blocks for Teaching Preschoolers with Special Needs represents an important step in this understanding for several reasons. First, it acknowledges the need for a variety of instructional approaches when working with children with a range of special needs. Second, it provides tools and guidance on how to decide what kind of instruction is appropriate and how to implement that instruction. Third, it puts instruction in the context of developmentally appropriate programming. In doing so, it avoids a common assumption that effective instruction and developmentally appropriate practice are somehow inconsistent with one another. Finally, *Building Blocks for Teaching Preschoolers with Special Needs* is written in such a way that professionals from many different kinds of backgrounds can use it. Conceptually, one could fit this model into a variety of different philosophical frameworks. On a practical level, this model for instruction could be implemented in the context of a variety of different curriculum approaches. The barriers to meaningful inclusion clearly cannot be addressed in a single book; however, the development and use of materials such as *Building Blocks for Teaching Preschoolers with Special Needs* will have a significant impact on overcoming some of the barriers to meaningful inclusion of young children with disabilities and other special needs in community-based settings.

Mary Louise Hemmeter, Ph.D.
University of Illinois at Urbana–Champaign

Acknowledgments

What does it mean to provide specialized instruction in an inclusive pre-school setting? We have been asking students, colleagues, and practition-ers this question; it is a question that they have been asking us; and it is the question that sparked the writing of this book. The answer is difficult to discover but very important. As we talked with students, parents, col-leagues, and practitioners, we realized the need for user-friendly materi-als that could help describe specialized instruction in inclusive settings, and, more important, help people implement it. That is the purpose of the Building Blocks model. We hope that teachers will use these resources to improve the quality and quantity of specialized instruction in inclusive preschool classrooms and that the improved specialized instruction will have a positive impact on the developmental outcomes of children with special needs.

Every book has many authors. Some of these authors are acknowl-edged publicly, and others may be unaware of the influence they have had on the text. First, we would like to thank those people who have been actively involved in the process. We have been lucky to work with a tal-ented group of co-authors, students, and colleagues throughout the de-velopment and field testing of Building Blocks.

The Building Blocks model grew out of work that was conducted by the Early Childhood Research Institute on Inclusion (ECRII), funded by the U.S. Department of Education. As Principal Investigator, Sam Odom assembled a multitalented group of investigators who committed to work together despite distance and methodological boundaries in order to un-derstand the barriers and facilitators of inclusion for young children with disabilities. We worked together for more than 5 years to collect, analyze, and make sense of a wealth of data about inclusion that parents, teachers, and children shared with us so generously.

To ensure that this study addressed the ethnic and cultural diversity of America's young children, a group of researchers in different regions of the country collaborated on the study. These researchers were affiliated with San Francisco State University, the University of Maryland, the University of North Carolina, the University of Washington, and Vanderbilt University in Nashville, Tennessee. The investigators included Paula Beckman, Marci Hanson, Eva Horn, Joan Lieber, Jules Marquart, and Ruth Wolery. We thank them for their spirit of inquiry and their collaboration.

We have also been very fortunate to have many colleagues, teachers, and mentors whose influence can easily be seen in the Building Blocks model. These people, to whom we extend our sincere thanks, include

- Diane Bricker, University of Oregon

- Mark Wolery, Vanderbilt University

- Phil Strain, University of Colorado at Denver and his colleagues at the ECRI at the University of Pittsburgh, including Diane Sainato, Ohio State University; Scott McConnell, University of Minnesota; and Howard Goldstein, Florida State University

- Judy Carta and her colleagues at the Juniper Garden Children's Project, University of Kansas

- Rebecca Fewell, University of Miami

- Don Baer, University of Kansas

- Susan Fowler, University of Illinois

- Robert Koegel, University of California at Santa Barbara, and Glen Dunlap, University of South Florida

- Marilou Hyson and the teachers and staff at the lab school at the University of Delaware

- the children, parents, and teachers at the Alice Hayden Preschool at the Experimental Education Unit, University of Washington

Finally, there have been a number of people who have helped us transform this project from notes to a manuscript to a published and user-friendly book. They include Joan Ronk and Margaret Brashers at the University of Washington and Heather Shrestha at Paul H. Brookes Publishing Co.

Susan R. Sandall and Ilene S. Schwartz
University of Washington, Seattle

For Casey

Using
the Model

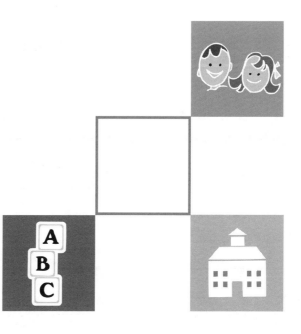

Introduction

This book describes practical examples of educational practices that support and enhance the inclusion of young children with disabilities and other special needs in community-based classrooms. It is designed for two primary audiences. First, teachers, caregivers, and other team members who work in community-based preschool classrooms that include children with disabilities and other special needs will find the book useful for their planning and teaching. Second, consulting teachers will find the book useful in their work with teachers in community-based classrooms.

This book contains the Building Blocks model—a set of educational practices designed to help teachers do a more effective job of including young children with disabilities and other special needs in preschool classrooms. It provides teachers with a variety of methods and strategies to ensure that children learn important skills in their preschool classrooms. These practices can be used to supplement the curriculum that the teacher currently uses. For example, these practices fit nicely with widely used curricula such as the Creative Curriculum (Dodge & Colker, 1992), High/Scope (Hohmann & Weikart, 1995), and the Assessment, Evaluation, and Programming System (AEPS) Curriculum for Three to Six Years, Second Edition (Bricker & Waddell, 2002).

IMPORTANT TERMS

The Building Blocks model uses a vocabulary that may already be familiar to many teachers. For the purposes of this book, however, it is important to clarify what these terms mean in the context of the model. The following sections define several important terms that are used throughout the book.

Inclusion

Inclusion is the active participation of young children with and without disabilities in the same classroom (e.g., Head Start, child care, preschool) and community settings. Within these settings, any services that children require to reach the individualized goals established for them by their families and a team of professionals should be provided (Filler, 1996). Inclusive early childhood classrooms should provide all children with the supports and related services needed to achieve valuable learning outcomes as well as to form and maintain productive social relationships with other children.

Children with Disabilities and Other Special Needs

The term *children with disabilities and other special needs* indicates children who are eligible for special education services and who have individualized education programs. It also refers to children who, for a variety of reasons, are struggling in their classrooms and need additional help or attention from their teachers.

Individualized Education Program

The *individualized education program (IEP)* is a document prepared for any student, ages 3 through 21, who is eligible for special education services. IEPs are required by the Individuals with Disabilities Education Act (IDEA) of 1990 (PL 101-476) and the Amendments of 1997 (PL 105-17). Each IEP contains 1) a statement of the child's present level of educational performance, 2) the child's annual goals and short-term objectives, 3) the special education and related services to be provided, 4) the extent to which the child will participate in the general education program, 5) the way in which the child's progress will be determined, and 6) the date of initiation and projected duration of services. For students age 14 and older, the IEP also contains a plan for making the transition from high school to adulthood. Children younger than 3 years and their families also have individual plans. These are called *individualized family service plans (IFSPs)*.

Community-Based Classrooms

The term *community-based classrooms* refers to the types of early childhood classroom programs that children may typically attend. These include child care centers, public school programs, Head Start programs, and private and cooperative preschools. Community-based classrooms do not include specialty clinics, laboratory classrooms, or other specialized schools.

Head Start

Head Start is a federally funded, comprehensive early childhood program that serves children from low-income families. Head Start programs reserve at least 10% of their enrollments for children with disabilities.

Related Services

Related services include physical, occupational, and speech therapy; psychological services; and others that a child with a disability may require to receive the greatest benefit from his or her education. Such services are provided by or under the supervision of certified or licensed individuals (e.g., speech-language therapist, child psychologist).

Team

Special education and related services are provided by a team. The *team* consists of family members and professionals who work together to plan and implement the child's educational program.

Early Childhood Education

In this book, *early childhood education (ECE)* refers to educational programs and activities for young children ages 3 through 6 years. The *ECE teacher* is an individual with training and preparation in child development and other content areas related to the education of young children. This individual may have certification in general early childhood education.

Early Childhood Special Education

In this book, *early childhood special education (ECSE)* refers to educational programs, activities, and services for young children with known or suspected disabilities who are ages 3 through 6 years. ECSE is guided by the requirements of federal and state policies as well as by research on effective educational practices. The *ECSE teacher* is an individual with additional specialized training and preparation for working with young children with disabilities and other special needs. This individual may work directly with children or in a consulting role. Special certification or endorsement is often required.

THE CHILDREN

The descriptions of educational practices in this book are enriched by the stories of four children and their teachers.

Nhan is a 4-year-old Vietnamese American boy. He receives special education because of delays in his language and social skills. He attends a child care center five days a week from 7:30 AM to 6 PM. His parents speak both English and Vietnamese. Nhan and his brother and sister were cared for at home by their Vietnamese-speaking grandmother until Nhan was 2 years old. He then began attending the child care center. His child care teachers became concerned about some of his behaviors and recommended to his parents that he be evaluated. He was identified as being eligible for special education and related services when he was 3 years old. He continues to attend the child care center, and the school district provides an ECSE teacher and a speech-language therapist who visit his classroom once a week. There is one other child in his classroom who has an IEP, and another teacher comes to visit that child. Nhan's child care teachers use the Creative Curriculum (Dodge & Colker, 1992).

Tina is a 4-year-old Caucasian girl. She was diagnosed with Down syndrome and has mild to moderate delays in most areas of development. Tina has been enrolled in special programs since she was 2 months old. When she was an infant, home visitors came to her home to provide services. As a toddler, she went to a program at a child development clinic. When she turned 3 years old, she went to a preschool class at a public school. This year, her mother transferred her to the Head Start classroom at the neighborhood center. This is the same program that her older brothers attended. There is one other child in her classroom who has an IEP. An ECSE teacher and a speech-language therapist visit the classroom and work with the two children and the teachers once a week. Tina's teacher, Dolores, has taught in Head Start for several years. All of the classrooms and teachers in this program use the High/Scope curriculum (Hohmann & Weikart, 1995).

Samisha is a 5-year-old African American girl with cerebral palsy who lives with her parents, grandmother, and three older siblings. She is learning to use a walker and, when motivated, can move quite quickly. In the classroom, she most often moves around by scooting on the floor. Samisha is very social, and she loves to be the center of attention. Her language skills are slightly delayed, but she does not demonstrate any cognitive delays. Although

she is very interested in the other children in her class, she is not very successful in peer interactions. She has a hard time with taking turns and sharing materials. She has good dramatic play skills when she suggests the story but has trouble changing her behavior to conform with a plan suggested by another child. Samisha attends a public school preschool classroom that is team taught by ECE and ECSE teachers Gia and David. There are 15 children in the classroom: Nine of the children are typically developing, and six qualify for special education services. The teachers identify their curriculum as "teacher created" and use their vast collection of ECE activity books as resources.

 Drew is a 3-year-old Caucasian boy who lives with his parents and two brothers, one older and one younger. At 30 months, Drew was diagnosed with autism; he functions at a high level. He has good expressive language skills, although they are not age appropriate. He has an extensive vocabulary and can use multiword sentences to express wants and needs, but he rarely makes comments or engages in social conversation. Drew can play independently for a long period of time with a few preferred toys. His favorites are trains, Disney figurines, and markers. He has little interest and few skills with other materials. Some people may consider his play to be repetitive or stereotypical. Drew is not very interested in his brothers or the other children in his classroom. He is very attached to his mother and seeks her out for comfort and when he wants something. One of Drew's major challenges is his tantrums. He has a very difficult time following even simple adult directions and will often start to throw a tantrum if anyone says "no." Drew attends an integrated classroom in a public school. The head teacher is trained in ECSE. There are 15 children in his class: Nine children with disabilities, and six who are typically developing. This classroom configuration has been called reverse mainstreaming. The teacher uses the AEPS (Bricker & Waddell, 2002) in her classroom.

You will learn more about Nhan, Tina, Samisha, and Drew, their teachers, and their classmates as you use this book. Their stories and the practices described in the book are offered to provide you with the support, guidance, and practical suggestions for including children with disabilities and other special needs in your classroom, which can enhance the development and learning of all young children.

Chapter 2

The Building Blocks Model

The Building Blocks model evolved from many research activities and experiences in preschool classrooms. The model is guided by the goals of successful inclusion and improved outcomes for young children with disabilities and other special needs in community-based early childhood classrooms. Using this model, teachers can help all of their students participate, learn, and thrive in their preschool classrooms.

To accomplish this, teachers must match an individual child's goals and objectives with appropriate teaching methods and materials, decide what amount of help or assistance is needed by the child, provide this assistance, and determine whether the assistance was helpful. Fortunately, a number of people (e.g., therapists, other specialists) are available to help the teacher. All of the people involved with the child must work together.

In addition, the successful inclusion of young children is based on the assumption that the early childhood settings in which the model will be implemented are already high quality—places where children are nurtured and where their basic developmental needs are met. The first step in using the Building Blocks framework is to assess what is currently happening in the classroom using the *Quality Classroom Assessment Form* in Chapter 4. Find out if the basic features of a high-quality early childhood program are in place. *Assessment* is the process of gathering information for the purpose of making a decision. Assessment of the preschool classroom recognizes the influence of the environment on behavior. By assessing the classroom, the education team can gather information to help determine the extent to which the classroom environment is likely to facilitate children's development and learning. If the assessment reveals that important factors are not present or not helpful, the team can begin to plan changes in the environment.

Second, the education team starts to consider the individual goals and objectives of the children in their classroom. Using an activity matrix is an easy way to consider children's learning objectives when planning classroom activities and routines (see Chapter 4 for more details).

Third, the education team plans for those children who have IEPs or who have difficulty with participating in the classroom. Each child should have an individualized plan that takes into consideration his or her particular strengths, interests, and needs. Planning for a child who has disabilities, challenging behaviors, or other special learning needs requires thoughtful teamwork and may also require adaptations to the usual curriculum or more planned opportunities for the child to learn and practice new skills and behaviors.

Figure 1 depicts the Building Blocks model. There are four key components to the Building Blocks model. The foundation—a high-quality early childhood program—is important for all children. The remaining blocks—curriculum modifications; embedded learning opportunities; and explicit, child-focused instructional strategies—represent educational practices that may be appropriate for some children for some of their learning objectives. The model also indicates that intensity and specificity of the practices increase as the blocks become smaller. The following sections describe each of the Building Block components in more detail. These elements and assumptions provide the foundational context for the Building Blocks model.

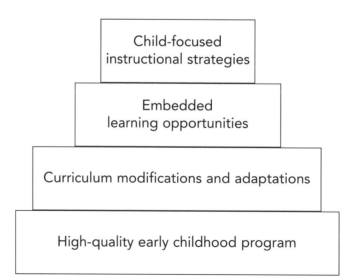

Figure 1. The Building Blocks Model.

HIGH-QUALITY EARLY CHILDHOOD PROGRAMS

A high-quality ECE program meets principles of developmentally appropriate practice that are based on current knowledge about child development and learning; the strengths, interests, and needs of each individual child in the group; and the social and cultural contexts in which the children live (Bredekamp & Copple, 1997). High-quality early childhood programs and developmentally appropriate practices are described in detail in a variety of resources (e.g., Bredekamp & Copple, 1997; Davis, Kilgo, & Gamel-McCormick, 1998). Research and experience have uncovered some necessary components of a developmentally appropriate learning environment:

- Engaging interactions
- A responsive and predictable environment
- Many opportunities for learning
- Teaching that is matched to the child and activity
- Developmentally appropriate materials, activities, and interactions
- Safe and hygienic practices
- Appropriate levels of child guidance

These features are necessary but may not be sufficient to meet the unique needs of young children with disabilities or other special needs. However, there are many ways that teachers can adjust their curricula to include all children.

CURRICULUM MODIFICATIONS

Teachers and other members of the team can make modifications, adaptations, and accommodations to classroom activities, routines, and learning areas in order to include children with disabilities and other special needs in the classroom and to enhance their participation.

Think about the four children described in Chapter 1. All of their teachers use curriculum modifications to address some of the children's individual learning objectives. For example, Nhan has a picture schedule to help him remember the daily schedule of events in his classroom. Tina takes a picture or toy with her to recall time so she has something to talk about. Samisha has a large block placed under her feet when sitting at the table to help her sit with better stability. Drew has his name written on his carpet square so that he knows where to sit at circle time.

A *curriculum modification* is a change made to the ongoing classroom activity or materials in order to achieve or maximize the child's participation. By increasing the child's participation in these activities and their playful interactions with toys and peers, the teacher can help the child take advantage of these opportunities to develop and learn. Of course, if the child is not able to learn through increased participation, the teacher must provide even more help or assistance. Chapter 5 provides more information and many examples of curriculum modifications.

EMBEDDED LEARNING OPPORTUNITIES

Teachers can increase or enhance children's learning time by embedding or integrating planned opportunities within the usual classroom activities and routines. These planned opportunities are called *embedded learning opportunities (ELO)*. Teachers identify the opportunities most salient to the individualized learning objectives for the child and take advantage of the child's interests by embedding short, systematic instructional interactions into the existing classroom activities and routines to enhance the child's learning. The teacher plans what he or she will say and do, and what materials he or she will use within these interactions.

 All of the children in this book have some of their learning objectives met through ELOs. Nhan gets planned practice at asking simple questions during arrival and snack times. Tina works on sorting by size in the dramatic play area with dishes and at the manipulatives area with the building toys. Samisha works on playing games with rules by playing games such as Lotto and CandyLand at the games table during her free-choice time. Drew gets additional learning opportunities to increase his play skills (using building toys) during free-choice time and small-group time.

The key characteristic of ELO is that the instructional interaction is planned and embedded, as naturally as possible, within an ongoing classroom activity or routine and that the effectiveness of instructional interaction is evaluated and modified if necessary. One distinction from the curriculum modification strategy is that the individualized objective for the child may be different from or more specific than the general goal of the activity or routine. For more information and examples of ELO, see Chapter 6.

EXPLICIT, CHILD-FOCUSED INSTRUCTIONAL STRATEGIES

Sometimes more explicit instruction is needed. Using *child-focused instructional strategies (CFIS),* ECE teachers or other specialists identify learning opportunities matched to the child's individual objective and provide planned, consistent, systematic instruction in order to teach specific skills, behaviors, or concepts. These skills, behaviors, or concepts may be ones that the child is not able to learn from the usual curriculum, even with modifications or ELOs; or these may be skills, behaviors, or concepts that are unique to the child.

All of the children's teachers use CFIS to address some of the children's learning objectives. Nhan receives instruction to increase his English vocabulary every morning. He asks a classmate to join him so that he can use his new words in conversation. Tina receives special instruction during her toileting time in which she works on unfastening and fastening her clothing. Samisha has a specially planned instructional program to teach her to sustain interactions with peers. It occurs every day at the beginning of free-choice time in the dramatic play area. Drew works on taking turns in conversation with peers at his small-group table. His teacher uses a systematic prompting strategy to increase the number and complexity of turns.

With CFIS, instructional interactions are even more systematic and more intensive than using modifications or embedding more opportunities. Although the use of modifications and ELOs allows the teacher to continue to make use of ongoing activities and routines, CFIS are used when the child's individual objectives and learning needs are such that the objective drives your planning. Sometimes, the child's learning activity may look different from the learning activity for other children in the classroom. Chapter 7 provides more information about CFIS and when to use them in the preschool classroom.

COLLABORATION

The effective use of the Building Blocks model requires that teachers and other team members work together through the process of *collaboration.* Collaboration is the cornerstone of effective inclusion. Collaborative teams hold shared beliefs, work toward common goals, have varying areas of expertise, use collaborative skills, and share the work. It is necessary to collaborate with family members as well as with other early childhood specialists in order to optimize child outcomes.

The four children are enrolled in a variety of classrooms with a variety of teaching arrangements, yet all of their teachers work collaboratively with others. These teams differ in membership depending on the goal or reason for the collaboration. Nhan's teachers, a consulting teacher, a speech-language therapist, and his parents meet regularly to plan for and discuss his progress in learning to communicate with adults and peers. Tina's teacher, Dolores, and the assistant teacher, Maggie, meet together at the end of every school day to talk about the day and to plan her next school day. Samisha's teachers and the physical therapist meet every other week to talk about her progress. Drew's teacher, Jennie; Jennie's assistant, Marlene; a speech-language therapist; an occupational therapist; Drew's mother; and a behavior specialist meet to develop a plan to decrease Drew's tantrums. For each of the children, their teachers, parents, related services providers, and school or program administrator meet together to develop the child's IEP.

Collaborative skills can be difficult to acquire and need lots of practice, but these skills are essential for successful inclusion. Chapter 3 provides more information and strategies to enhance collaboration among the people who care about young children.

SUMMARY

This chapter introduces the Building Blocks model. The aim of the model is to help teachers identify, plan, and use teaching strategies that provide individual children with the assistance they need to develop and learn within their preschool classrooms. Subsequent chapters offer more information about each of these teaching strategies.

Chapter 3

Keys to Collaboration

Collaboration is critical to the success of preschool inclusion. Preschool inclusion necessitates that people with different expertise in early childhood, special education, and specific children work together to develop creative approaches. Collaboration happens when people meet together as a team on a consistent basis to share information and to solve problems. Here are several key factors that make collaboration successful:

- Adequate time for the team to meet
- Respect for others' contributions
- Trust
- Effective communication
- Participation of all team members
- The ability to identify goals and develop strategies to meet them

HOW TO FORM A TEAM

When forming a team, it is helpful to first determine the team model, goal, and membership. Inclusion exists in many forms, and special education services use many different models based on where children with disabilities participate with other children (e.g., Head Start programs, child care centers, and public and private preschools) (Odom, Horn, et al., 1999).

In addition, the ways in which specialized services are designed and delivered may vary. Table 1 lists and describes some of these models.

Always ask "What goals will our team address?" Having shared goals is fundamental to a well-functioning team. Identification of team goals will also guide the team's membership. Table 2 lists several examples.

Team members include classroom assistants or paraprofessionals; related services personnel such as physical therapists, occupational therapists, and speech-language pathologists; the child's parents or guardians; and the program's administrator. Team members may vary depending on the immediate goal or purpose for meeting together as a team. For goals such as IEP planning, the team may be rather large. For other goals, such as ongoing curriculum planning, the team is smaller.

Strategies for Meeting as a Team

Teachers say that finding time to meet is one of the most difficult problems they face. Here are some ideas that teachers have shared for meeting times:

- Some teachers like to meet before the children arrive or after the children leave.
- Others meet during naptime.
- In one program, all of the children had motor time with the adapted physical education teacher once a week. During that weekly time, the other staff members held a team meeting.
- In one district, schools had an early release day once each week. That time was used for team meetings.

Telephone and e-mail can be useful communication tools to assist in the collaboration process. However, it's important that the team has some face-to-face meeting times, as these enhance the development of trust and

Table 1. Inclusion models

Service model	Description
Team teaching	An early childhood education (ECE) teacher and an early childhood special education (ECSE) teacher jointly plan for and implement instruction in a classroom that includes children with and without disabilities.
Consultation	The ECE teacher provides most of the instruction in the inclusive classroom. An ECSE teacher comes to the classroom to consult on a regular basis.
Reverse mainstreaming	An ECSE teacher is the lead teacher in a classroom that includes children with and without disabilities.
Integrated activities	The ECE teacher and the ECSE teacher have separate classes. They bring the children together for joint activities on a regular basis.

Table 2. Examples of identifying team goals

Model	Goal	Team members
Team teaching	Planning learning activities for the classroom	Early childhood education (ECE) teacher
		Early childhood special education (ECSE) teacher
Team teaching	Developing Samisha's individualized education program	Samisha's parents, ECE teacher, ECSE teacher, physical therapist, speech-language pathologist, program director
Consultation	Modifying child care center activities for Nhan	ECE teacher, consulting ECSE teacher, consulting speech-language pathologist, assistant teacher

understanding of others' perspectives. In particular, e-mail should be used with care because it can be difficult to discern the writer's tone and true meaning.

How to Structure a Meeting

Once a team is organized and has established meeting times, the general structure or framework of meetings should be devised to ensure that the team meetings run smoothly and that tasks are accomplished. The first step is to choose roles for *this* team meeting. These roles should rotate from one meeting to the next. At each team meeting, choose a facilitator. The facilitator's tasks during the meeting include helping create the agenda and assigning times to agenda items, keeping the meeting moving and on topic, and soliciting participation from each team member. Each meeting also needs a recorder to note what happens during the meeting, including all decisions that are made, and to record who is responsible for specific follow-up activities. Finally, every meeting needs a timekeeper to make sure that the meeting starts and ends on time and to let team members know when time is up for discussing each item on the agenda.

The second step is to set the agenda. The facilitator takes the initiative in setting the agenda. He or she begins by summarizing the results of the last meeting as set forth by the last meeting's recorder. Then, the facilitator identifies the purpose for this meeting and works with the team to decide what should be discussed in order to achieve the purpose. The minutes of the last meeting can serve as a prompt for remembering any unfinished business.

The third step is the discussion of the agenda items. This should take up the greatest portion of the meeting time, and, ideally, everyone in the meeting participates during this step. The facilitator should solicit participation from anyone who is being quiet. Sometimes this may mean encouraging team members to confront areas of disagreement. The facilitator is also responsible for keeping team members moving toward the stated purpose of the meeting and redirecting team members who digress from the topic. Toward the end of this step, the facilitator should restate, reflect, and summarize the discussion, and if a decision is imminent, he or she should summarize the decision for the team. This allows team members to hear the decision articulated in someone else's words and can help clarify any miscommunication.

The final step is ending the meeting. During this step, the facilitator, with the help of the recorder, makes sure that all team members know what tasks need to be accomplished before the team gets together for the next meeting. More information about how to structure a meeting can be found in Hunter, Bailey, and Taylor (1995).

Steps in Achieving Your Team's Goal

Before teams begin to work toward their goal, they should be sure that all team members share an understanding of what the goal means and how they will know when the goal has been met. For example, an ECE teacher and ECSE teacher are working together using the team teaching model; their goal is to plan learning activities for the classroom. They first need to agree about what "Plan learning activities for the classroom" means to them. Some of the questions the team members might ask themselves are

- Will we write lesson plans together?
- Will we be responsible for jointly delivering the instruction?
- Will the ECE teacher plan each activity and the ECSE teacher plan the modifications?
- Will the ECE teacher and the ECSE teacher take turns and plan independently for certain activities or days?

There are no right answers. The point of this exercise is for the team members to agree about the meaning of the goal. This team may decide to meet each Friday afternoon and produce joint lesson plans for the following week. They will know they've met their goal each Friday.

PROBLEM SOLVING

Team members often must identify and solve problems that arise in trying to meet the goal. These problem-solving steps are described in detail by Friend and Cook (2000) and by Pugach and Johnson (1995):

1. Identify the problem.
2. Generate solutions.

3. Evaluate the solutions.

4. Implement the solution you choose.

5. Evaluate the outcome.

Tina's team is made up of her ECE teacher, Dolores; the assistant teacher, Maggie; the consulting ECSE teacher; and the consulting speech-language pathologist. They are using the consultation model, and their goal is to include Tina in all classroom activities. They are meeting because Tina often refuses to walk from the playground to the classroom, which constitutes a barrier to the team's expressed goal.

The first step, problem identification, is probably the most important step in the process. The team needs to define terms, as was done in the goal statement, so that all team members are in agreement.

When this team came together, they needed to ask questions such as

- *How does Tina refuse?*

- *What does she do and say?*

- *How long does the situation last?*

- *Does it happen at any other time?*

- *What do the adults do?*

Once the team members reach a consensus regarding the problem, the next step is generating solutions. Friend and Cook (2000) described three different approaches that can be used to generate solutions: brainstorming, brainwriting, and nominal group technique. These approaches allow the team to generate many potential solutions to the problem before the team settles on one solution.

During *brainstorming*, team members verbally call out potential solutions. No solution is evaluated during the brainstorming stage, and the team members state as many solutions as they can think of. *Brainwriting* is similar, but each team member writes down potential solutions and then shares them with the group. Using the *nominal group technique*, each team member writes several potential solutions. Then, each team member shares one solution at a time and takes turns sharing until all solutions have been presented. The recorder lists each solution, and team members rate each solution on a scale from one to five.

Now the team is ready to evaluate the potential solutions that have been generated. One way to do this is to list or describe the positive and negative features of each solution. Team members should remember that some solutions may require additional authority (e.g., allocating funds, changing job responsibilities). The team should select one of the possible solutions to use during their problem-solving session.

Here are the solutions generated by Tina's team:

- *Pick her up and walk with her*
- *Let Tina ride in a wagon*
- *Use a peer buddy to walk with Tina*
- *Let Tina carry a favorite toy back to class*
- *Make sure that Tina's favorite activity is available when she gets to class*
- *Let Tina walk with her favorite teacher*
- *Wait with her without talking until she stands up and walks to class*
- *Use some kind of tangible reinforcer and give to Tina when she gets to class*

Following their discussion of the positives and negatives of each potential solution, the team decided to try using a peer-buddy system. Next, they assigned tasks to be accomplished:

- *Dolores will talk with a few classmates to recruit them to be Tina's partner.*
- *Dolores or Maggie will remind Tina at the end of playground time that it is time for her to pick a buddy.*
- *The consulting ECSE teacher will make a picture card that has photos of Tina's buddies for her to choose from.*
- *The consulting ECSE teacher will make a simple data collection chart.*

The final step in problem solving is to implement the selected solution, collect data, and at the end of some specified period of time, evaluate to see if the solution worked. If it did, the team will continue with it. If not, the team will meet again and decide on another option. The team can use the *Evaluation Worksheet* (see Chapter 4) to keep track of their plan and to evaluate it. In addition, the planning forms in Appendix A, *The Team Agenda* and the *Problem-Solving Worksheet,* can be used by the team.

Chapter 4

Getting Started

The Building Blocks model is designed to help teachers identify concerns in the classroom and plan strategies for helping a child develop and learn when he or she is having trouble with meeting his or her individual learning objectives. The format is appropriate for any child who has repeated challenges in the classroom. This may be because the child is not learning or because the child is displaying excessive behaviors that interfere with the child's own learning or the learning of others. The Building Blocks model can also be used for children who are identified for special education and have IEPs.

This chapter describes the procedures for using the Building Blocks model in preschool classrooms. These step-by-step procedures guide the team from the initial concern (e.g., how to teach the IEP objectives, what to do about a challenging behavior) to a useful plan. The goal is to help the team transform the IEP, other individual plan, or concern into actual teaching and learning opportunities in the classroom. This chapter will help the team

- Assess the classroom to ensure that it provides a high-quality learning environment for all children
- Identify the classroom schedule
- Gather information on children's individual learning objectives
- Assess the classroom learning needs of a child who concerns the team

- Clarify the concerns
- Construct a *Child Activity Matrix* that shows when the plan will be used
- Implement the plan
- Evaluate the plan

Numerous forms are included to help teams reach these goals. Although many forms are provided, teams should only use those that work for them—it is not necessary to use each of these forms. This chapter contains filled-out forms; blank forms that teams can photocopy and use are in Appendix A.

STEP 1: ASSESSING THE QUALITY OF YOUR CLASSROOM

In the Building Blocks model, the specialized practices are built on the foundation of a high-quality early childhood program. The first step is for the teacher or classroom team (i.e., the people who know the classroom well) to assess the preschool classroom for 10 basic quality indicators using the *Quality Classroom Assessment Form*. It's especially helpful to list examples for each of the 10 indicators. The results of the assessment tell the team if the classroom is interesting and engaging to children, offers a balance of activities and learning arrangements, and provides both physical and emotional security. Tina's teachers completed the form for their classroom (see Figure 2). (A blank form is available in Appendix A.)

Some teachers or teams may already use another rating form to assess the classroom environment—for example, the Early Childhood Environment Rating Scale–Revised (ECERS-R; Harms, Clifford, & Cryer, 1998) or as part of an accreditation process. Any of these assessments will yield the necessary information.

What to Do

Strive to make your classroom a vibrant learning place for all children. If any foundational features are weak or missing, describe actions that the team can take to address the problem. The Classroom Action Worksheet (see Figure 3) can be used if you answered "no" or "not sure" to any items on the classroom assessment form. Team members may also use their own experience along with classroom resource books to enhance the classroom. (See the resource list in Appendix B). Next, the team implements these actions. This will help ensure a high-quality environment for all the children in the classroom.

Quality Classroom Assessment Form

Date: 1/16/02

Classroom: Head Start classroom

Team members: Dolores Sherman (teacher)   Maggie Ong (assistant teacher)

Goal: Assess the classroom environment

Indicator	Yes	No	Not sure	Examples
1. Do children spend most of their time playing and working with materials or with other children?	X			Children are busy and active most of the time.
2. Do children have access to various activities throughout the day?	X			We schedule different sorts of activities.
3. Do teachers work with individual children, small groups, and the whole group at different times during the day?	X			Scheduled small groups and snack; meeting times with whole group; individual time during plan-do-recall
4. Is the classroom decorated with children's original artwork, their own writing, and stories they've dictated?		X		Lots of artwork; no writing
5. Do children learn within meaningful (i.e., relevant to their interests and experiences) contexts?	X			Classroom organized for High/Scope, learning centers, projects based on children's ideas

(continued)

Figure 2. Quality Classroom Assessment Form, as completed by Tina's teachers.

Figure 2. *(continued)*

Quality Classroom Assessment Form

(continued)

Indicator	Yes	No	Not sure	Examples
6. Do children work on projects and have periods of time to play and explore?	X			Small-group projects; plan-do-recall at their own pace
7. Do children have an opportunity to play and explore?	X			Always scheduled
8. Do teachers read books to children individually or in small groups throughout the day?		X		Read to large group, not all are interested; book area is not very popular
9. Is the curriculum adapted for those who are ahead as well as those who need additional help?			X	We use High/Scope. We're not sure we're meeting all of Tina's needs.
10. Do the children and their families feel safe and secure within their early childhood program?	X			Most children are happy when they arrive; lots of parents at parent activities

Notes: _We need to complete the Classroom Action Worksheet for Questions 4, 8, and 9._

_____

_____

_____

Classroom Action Worksheet

Date: __01/17/02__

Team members: __Dolores and Maggie__

Indicator	What's the problem?	What can we do?	Who will do it?	By when?
4. Class decor	We have artwork but no writing.	Ask children to talk about their art. Write their stories and post with their art.	Dolores Maggie	Start on Monday and continue
8. Book reading	We have storytime for the whole group. Not everyone listens or participates.	Make the library corner more interesting. Have an adult in this center to read to small groups and one-to-one. Add props to storytime.	Maggie will fix the library corner and volunteer in the library on Wednesdays. Dolores will get new props.	Next week
9. Adapted curriculum	Tina doesn't seem to be making progress in her fine motor skills.	Ask the consulting special education teacher for more information and to break down the objectives into smaller parts. Ask her to demonstrate for us.	Dolores will talk with the consulting teacher and schedule a time during the visit so that she can show us.	In 2 weeks

Figure 3. Classroom Action Worksheet, as completed by Tina's teachers.

STEP 2: PLANNING THE CLASSROOM SCHEDULE

One way to help ensure a safe and secure learning environment for children is to have a schedule. A schedule provides a predictable routine for children and should

- Be divided into time segments that are appropriate to the children's needs and abilities
- Offer a balance of active and quiet times
- Provide times for large- and small-group activities and time to play alone or with others
- Include outdoor time
- Offer a balance of child-initiated activities and teacher-directed activities
- Include adequate time for routines (e.g., toileting and snacks) and transitions
- Maximize teaching and learning time and minimize waiting time

What to Do

If the classroom does not have a consistent schedule or if the current schedule is not working, your team should work together to design a new classroom schedule. (See Davis, Kilgo, & Gamel-McCormick, 1998, for ideas. Other resources are available in Appendix B.)

STEP 3: PLANNING FOR AN INDIVIDUAL CHILD

With an inviting classroom environment and a consistent schedule, the next step is to plan for an individual child. Teams must gather each child's current *individual learning objectives.* For some children, objectives come directly from the IEP. The team should break down an IEP objective into smaller, more manageable objectives. A learning or behavioral objective has the following components:

- The learner
- The behavior
- The criterion (i.e., how many, how often, how much of the time, or how long)
- Under what conditions

Here are some individual learning objectives for Tina and Drew: When given a mixed group of objects, Tina will sort all of the objects into smaller groups according to some physical attribute (e.g., color, size) six different times using six different sets of materials (e.g., colored dishes, big and little cars).
During free-play times, Drew will demonstrate five new play skills (e.g., painting, doing puzzles, building with blocks) on three different occasions for at least 10 minutes each time.

Sometimes a teacher's concerns about a child seem so overwhelming that it's difficult to clarify the actual problem areas, which makes it even more difficult to design an effective plan. For example, a child may have so many objectives on his or her IEP that the team wonders how they can possibly find more time to teach the child. Or another child may display so many challenges in the classroom (e.g., running away, grabbing toys, yelling) that the adults feel that they are spending all their time trying to regain order.

The Child Assessment Worksheet can help pinpoint your concerns for a particular child and link those concerns to the classroom schedule and ongoing activities. This form guides the collection of information to determine how the child is doing within the context of the classroom and whether the child's learning needs are being met.

Drew's teacher and the rest of the classroom team met together and used the Child Assessment Worksheet to help them plan for Drew (see Figure 4). They wanted to incorporate his IEP goals within the classroom activities and routines and to better understand his challenging behaviors.

What to Do

The team should work together to complete the worksheet. First, fill out the first column with the classroom schedule. Then, in the next column, list classroom expectations for children during each scheduled event. For example, at snack time, do you expect children to find their seat, remain seated, ask for food and drink, and clean up? Do you expect children to do this all by themselves or with directions from the teacher? Each classroom will be different. Doing this as a team helps ensure that all of the adults have similar expectations for children and activities during the day. In the third column, rate the child's current performance during each of the scheduled activities and routines. Is the child's current performance a

Child Assessment Worksheet

Date: __01/17/02__

Teacher's name: __Jennie__   Child's name: __Drew__

Classroom activities	Classroom expectations	Child's level of performance
Arrival	Be able to wait with other children until everyone gets off the bus. Walk to class with the group without holding the teacher's hand.	Strength _____ Average _____ Area of concern __X__
Circle time	Sit on his mat. Watch the teacher. Participate in songs and finger plays.	Strength _____ Average __X__ Area of concern _____
Small-group time	Participate in planned activity. Share materials. Sit at the table.	Strength _____ Average _____ Area of concern __X__
Free choice time	Try activities in the different areas. Play, with minimal teacher support.	Strength _____ Average _____ Area of concern __X__

(continued)

Figure 4. A Child Assessment Worksheet for Drew.

28

Child Assessment Worksheet

Date: 01/17/02

Teacher's name: Jennie   Child's name: Drew (page 2)

Classroom activities	Classroom expectations	Child's level of performance
Clean up and transition	Put away toys when asked by teacher. Stop playing when asked.	Strength _____ Average _____ Area of concern __X__
Snack time	Sit at table. Try food. Interact with peers as appropriate.	Strength _____ Average _____ Area of concern __X__
Outdoor time	Run and play. Explore equipment. Share toys.	Strength __X__ Average _____ Area of concern _____
Departure	Follow teacher directions.	Strength _____ Average _____ Area of concern __X__

strength, average (not a concern), or an area of concern? It's best if the team does this together. It allows the team members to share their perspectives and come to a consensus.

STEP 4: CLARIFY THE PROBLEM, ISSUE, OR CONCERN

After compiling a picture of the child's performance throughout the day, think about the following questions: What are the areas of concern? When does the child do well? When do the problems or concerns occur? Which concerns have the highest priority? The Planning Worksheet helps to plan a course of action for meshing classroom concerns with a child's IEP objectives. This worksheet is designed to guide the team's discussion of the individual child. The team aims for careful description of the concern (e.g., grabbing materials) and the team's current response. This leads to a problem-solving discussion and the team's best ideas for addressing the concern.

What to Do

In the first column, list the classroom activities that are areas of concern for the child in descending order of priority. These come from the Child Assessment Worksheet.

After completing the Child Assessment Worksheet for Drew, the team identified three scheduled activities that were areas of concern (see Figure 5). After discussing Drew's needs, his IEP, the needs of the other children in the classroom, and the available resources, the team decided to focus their attention on three scheduled activities: small-group time, free-choice time, and transitions. They reasoned that if they and Drew could be successful during these times, then Drew would have many more opportunities to learn and participate in the classroom.

In the second column, describe the problem or concern as carefully as you can. Make your description specific to the classroom activity. Write down exactly what the child does. Sometimes it's important to capture what the child doesn't do as well. For example, one child stands or sits by her cubbie during free-choice time but never chooses an activity. Another child makes choices and plays creatively with toys but never speaks to the other children; he only nods and points. Again, the team should identify these issues together. In the third column, describe what the

Planning Worksheet

Date: 01/17/02

Teacher's name: Jennie

Child's name: Drew

This planning guide will help you collect more specific information for areas of concern for specific children. Using the *Child Assessment Worksheet*, identify three activities on which you would like to focus your attention. Once you identify the problem, collecting information is the next step for instructional planning for children in inclusive settings.

(Key: CM = curriculum modification; ELO = embedded learning opportunity; CFIS = child-focused instructional strategy)

Activities	Define concern	What are you currently doing?	Ideas for instruction
Small group	Drew grabs materials from children who are next to him and needs a great deal of adult attention in order to stay engaged with the activity.	Drew has an assigned seat at small group, and a teacher always sits next to him. When materials are put on the table, he often grabs the most preferred ones and won't share. Then a teacher must intervene.	CM _X_ ELO _____ CFIS _____ Describe: Drew will work independently for at least 5 minutes and respect boundaries telling him what materials are his. We will put his materials on a tray and praise him when he is engaged with his materials.
Free choice	Drew will play for a long time with preferred materials but refuses to even try the majority of the materials in the classroom.	Drew is asked to make a choice about where he wants to play. He almost always chooses the trains and cars. When teachers suggest that he make a new choice, he often throws a tantrum. Teachers usually let him stay where he is.	CM _X_ ELO _____ CFIS _____ Describe: Drew will go to at least three areas during free choice time. We will make sure that trains is the last area he goes to and that he can spend the longest time there. Use a picture schedule.
Transitions	Drew does not respond to a transition signal if he is at a preferred activity. If he is at a nonpreferred activity, he runs or wanders around the classroom.	A teacher goes to Drew, repeats the instruction, and physically helps him with the transition. He often has a tantrum.	CM _____ ELO _____ CFIS _X_ Describe: Drew will use a picture schedule. We will go through the picture schedule at the beginning of the day. At each transition, we will show him the schedule and repeat the instructions.

Figure 5. A Planning Worksheet for Drew.

team currently does. What kind of assistance is provided (e.g., physical help, repeated instructions)? Is it consistent? What sorts of environmental supports (e.g., pictures, models) are currently in place? If the concern is a challenging behavior, how do the adults and children respond to the child?

In the fourth column, indicate your plan or your ideas for assistance or instruction. Use collaboration skills (e.g., sharing ideas, listening, problem solving) to arrive at your plan (see also Chapter 3). Chapters 5, 6, and 7 contain more information about using curriculum modifications, ELO, and CFIS.

These worksheets require teams to discuss and summarize the child's special learning needs, including the child's IEP objectives as well as the concerns identified through an assessment of the child's current level of participation in the classroom.

 Drew's team—his classroom teacher, her assistant, the speech-language therapist, the occupational therapist, and the behavior specialist—met together after school to discuss the results of their assessment and to figure out a plan. Drew's mother wasn't able to join them that day. She sent her notes and asked that Drew's teacher, Jennie, call her at the end of the meeting. Drew's team summarized current elements of his level of participation:

- *Transitions are difficult for Drew.*

- *He grabs materials and doesn't participate appropriately in small-group activities.*

- *He has a limited number of preferred play activities; this limits his participation and learning during free-choice time.*

His team also listed his current IEP objectives:

- *Interact appropriately with materials during small-group activities*

- *Follow teacher-given instructions*

- *Respond to others' initiations of conversational topics*

- *Share or exchange objects during play*

- *Demonstrate five new play skills (e.g., painting, doing puzzles, building)*

- *Respond appropriately to general knowledge questions (e.g., How old are you?)*

Because Drew's classroom has several children with special needs, the team wanted to use teaching strategies that were fairly simple but also likely to be successful. They realized that the different adults had tried different approaches and that none of them had been very good at follow-through. The team knew they needed to be more consistent.

Drew's team decided that a curriculum modification was likely to help Drew keep his materials organized and his hands to himself during small-group time. They also decided that another curriculum modification—a picture schedule—could be used to help Drew participate in free-choice time and to make transitions. As an ELO, the pictures also will be used as a prompt to teach Drew to follow directions. As part of this discussion, the team will decide how they will know if they and Drew have made progress. Although Drew's team is large, the same process could be done by Jennie and the consulting teacher for all other children with special needs in the classroom.

STEP 5: CONSTRUCT AN ACTIVITY MATRIX

An *activity matrix* helps teachers and teams ensure that teaching occurs. It's difficult to individualize for one child within a busy preschool classroom. A matrix reminds the team of 1) their planned schedule, 2) the number of children and the number of activities, 3) the number of adults who are available to assist, and 4) which activities require adult monitoring. These reminders help ensure that the teaching of important objectives is planned and implemented. They also help the teacher and the team use their time and resources in the best ways possible.

An activity matrix can be constructed in a variety of ways. Some teams photocopy the form provided and write in the information for their class. Other teams use a computer to construct an activity matrix. Other teams like to draw a large matrix on art paper and use adhesive notes to fill in the cells. Teams should use what works best for them. It's important for classroom staff to actively participate in creating the activity matrix. When people simply read a matrix prepared by someone else, there's a reduced chance that they will actually remember and implement the planned practices.

What to Do

To make a matrix for one child, write the classroom schedule down the left-hand column. Write the child's name at the top *and* write the child's current objectives across the first row. To make a matrix for several children or the whole class, write the classroom schedule down the left-hand column, then put the names of the children across the first row. (Activity matrices are used throughout the book as basic planning forms. Look at them carefully. You will see variations of the activity matrix for one child, many children, and for collecting information about children's progress.) Use the following codes for the matrices:

CM = curriculum modification

ELO = embedded learning opportunity

CFIS = child-focused instructional strategy

Figure 6 is a Child Activity Matrix for Tina. Figure 7 is a Classroom Activity Matrix for Tina's classroom, which includes two children with IEPs, Tina and Tyrone, and a third child with challenging behaviors, Ricky. Figure 8 is a Child Activity Matrix for Drew.

STEP 6: IMPLEMENT AND EVALUATE THE PLAN

And now comes the fun part. Try out the plan you've developed for the student in the classroom for at least a week. Happily, plans often work—for example, the child is captivated by the new toy and joins the group; using a favorite colored paper entices another child to the writing center; or pairing a child with a buddy solves the problem of returning at recess. But other times, the plans just don't work. It's the other children who like the new toy, the preferred color has no effect, and now you have two children who dawdle after recess. If the plan doesn't work well, try it for one more day. Use verbal reminders to help the child understand what's expected. Talk up the new toy, the new colored paper, or any other change you've implemented. Make it special. Then observe carefully. Some children need to get comfortable with the change before they try it out. Try again. Remember that what the team was doing before did not work either. Teaching is a constant process of observing, assessing, making teaching plans, and trying them out. The excitement is in figuring it out as well as in the child's accomplishment.

What to Do

At the end of the trial period, answer the questions on the Evaluation Worksheet: Did the plan work? What will you do next week? This worksheet suggests three ways to collect evaluation information: counts, notes, and permanent products. *Counts* mean that you record or tally each time the child exhibits the behavior (also called *event sampling*), or you record or tally the occurrence or nonoccurrence of the behavior during a specified time period (also called *time sampling*). Counting works well for recording the occurrence of behaviors: movements that have clear beginnings and ends such as jumping, buttoning, or asking for more.

Notetaking involves making a written record of the child's performance. You can write down your notes as the behavior occurs or shortly afterward. Notes can be useful for recording more continuous behaviors. Notes also provide information about qualitative aspects of the event such as the child's approach to a toy, persistence, and interest. Always date your notes.

Permanent products means that you collect a sample of the child's work. Ways to do this include keeping drawings or other artwork, making audiotapes or videotapes, or taking photographs. It's helpful to write a

Child Activity Matrix

Teacher's name: _____Dolores_____   Date: ___1/17/02___   Child's name: ___Tina___

Key: CM = curriculum modification; ELO = embedded learning opportunity; CFIS = child-focused instructional strategy

	Use short phrases to request and comment	Use words to recall actions or events	Respond appropriately during transitions	Share or exchange objects with peers	Sort objects by variety of attributes	Fit things together and take them apart	Unfasten and fasten clothing (e.g., snaps, zipper on coat)
Arrival			CM—use picture cards				CFIS—backward chain
Recall		CM—use picture cards					
Planning	CM—picture of schedule of classes						
Work				CM—paired activities	ELO—sort dishes, sort building toys	CM—preferred activities	

(continued)

Figure 6. A Child Activity Matrix for Tina.

Child Activity Matrix

Teacher's name: _____Dolores_____   Date: _____1/17/02_____   Child's name: _____Tina (page 2)_____

Key: CM = curriculum modification; ELO = embedded learning opportunity; CFIS = child-focused instructional strategy

	Use short phrases to request and comment	Use words to recall actions or events	Respond appropriately during transitions	Share or exchange objects with peers	Sort objects by variety of attributes	Fit things together and take them apart	Unfasten and fasten clothing (e.g., snaps, zipper on coat)
Snack	CM—preferred foods						
Toileting							CFIS—backward chain
Small and large group time	CM—preferred materials			CM—paired activities	ELO—plan for sorting activities in small group		
Departure							ELO—practice fastening

Classroom Activity Matrix

Date: ___1/17/02___

Teacher's name: ___Dolores and Maggie___

	Tina	Tyrone	Ricky				
Arrival	CM—use picture cards	CFIS—identify name	CM—use picture schedule (all day)				
Recall	CM—use words and picture cards	ELO—use descriptive words					
Planning	CM—request and comment						
Work	CM—share; fit together ELO—sorting	CM—play near peers; use preferred materials	CM—use picture schedule and timer				

Key: CM = curriculum modification; ELO = embedded learning opportunity; CFIS = child-focused instructional strategy

37

Figure 7. A Classroom Activity Matrix for Tina, Tyrone, and Ricky.

(continued)

Classroom Activity Matrix

Date: __1/17/02__

Teacher's name: __Dolores and Maggie (page 2)__

Key: CM = curriculum modification; ELO = embedded learning opportunity; CFIS = child-focused instructional strategy

	Tina	Tyrone	Ricky				
Snack time	CM—requests; use preferred food						
Toileting	CFIS— backward chain						
Small and large group time	CM—requests; share; ELO— sorting	ELO—use descriptive words					
Departure	ELO— fastening						

Child Activity Matrix

Teacher's name: ___Jennie___   Date: ___1/17/02___   Child's name: ___Drew___

Key: CM = curriculum modification; ELO = embedded learning opportunity; CFIS = child-focused instructional strategy

	Interact with materials	Follow teacher-given instructions	Respond to others' conversational topics	Share or exchange objects	Demonstrate five new play skills	Respond to general knowledge questions
Arrival			ELO—most to least prompt			
Circle time						CM—invisible support (follow preferred peer)
Small group	CM—environmental support			CFIS—model, differential reinforcement	CFIS—model, differential reinforcement	
Work	CM—preferred activity is final					

(continued)

Figure 8.   A Child Activity Matrix for Drew.

Child Activity Matrix

Teacher's name: _Jennie_   Date: _1/17/02_   Child's name: _Drew (page 2)_

Key: CM = curriculum modification; ELO = embedded learning opportunity; CFIS = child-focused instructional strategy

	Interact with materials	Follow teacher-given instructions	Respond to others' conversational topics	Share or exchange objects	Demonstrate five new play skills	Respond to general knowledge questions
Snack	CM—environmental support					ELO—most to least prompt
Outdoor time				ELO—differential reinforcement		
Transitions		ELO—picture as prompt				
Departure						

Evaluation Worksheet

Teacher's name: ___Jennie___   Date: ___1/17/02___   Child's name: ___Drew___

Concern	Plan	Evaluation information
Grabs materials from others and needs a great deal of adult attention	Work for 5 minutes. Give Drew his own tray and materials. Praise him when he is participating.	Counts ___ Notes _X_ Products ___ M—took Molly's glue bottle; Th—no grabbing today Did the plan work? (Yes) No What will you do next week? Drew is participating more fully. Continue with the plan.
Plays for a long time with preferred materials but refuses to try other materials	Use a picture schedule with four areas, and make the final area trains and cars. Use a timer and strive for 7 minutes in each of the first three areas.	Counts ___ Notes _X_ Products ___ W—at the sensory table for 3 min, books 4 min, art 6 min. (Drew did great in the art center!) Did the plan work? (Yes) No What will you do next week? Continue
Throws a tantrum or wanders at transition times	Give instructions for making the transition. Show the picture. Prompt using slight physical assistance.	Counts _X_ Notes ___ Products ___ (record data on Drew's transition chart) Did the plan work? (Yes) No What will you do next week? Continue

41

Figure 9. An Evaluation Worksheet for Drew.

comment and the date and attach these to the product. All of these per-formance records can be kept and organized in the child's *portfolio*, a col-lection of a child's work that demonstrates the child's efforts, progress, and achievements over time.

Collect information in the way that works best for you and your classroom. The point is to regularly collect the information. Remember, it can tell you that the child is learning and that your teaching makes the difference. Figure 9 contains a completed Evaluation Worksheet for Drew.

SUMMARY

This chapter introduces you to the Building Blocks framework for includ-ing children with disabilities or other special needs in your classroom. Successful inclusion means that all of the children in the classroom par-ticipate, learn, and thrive. Before you can make, implement, and evaluate a plan, you need to become more familiar with the rest of the book. Deciding whether to use curriculum modifications, ELOs, or CFIS takes practice. There are no hard and fast rules. It depends on the child, the ob-jective, and the classroom. It's a team decision. Use collaboration skills, and problem solve. Here are some helpful tips:

- If the child needs a little bit of help, try a curriculum modifica-tion.

- If the child needs a lot of assistance and direction, try a CFIS.

- If the need lies somewhere in between, try ELOs.

- If your evaluation data tell you that your first attempt didn't work, try again.

Teaching Strategies

Chapter 5

Curriculum Modifications

A *curriculum modification* is a change to the ongoing classroom activity or materials in order to facilitate or maximize the child's participation. The underlying notion is that through an increase in the child's participation in these activities as well as the child's playful interactions with toys and peers, the child can take advantage of these opportunities and consequently develop and learn.

Curriculum modifications should be thought of as easy-to-implement "interventions" that require thought and planning but should not require additional resources. In fact, many teachers regularly make curriculum modifications without identifying them as such.

Drew had a hard time with settling down in one spot at the beginning of large-group activities. The children in Drew's classroom all use carpet squares to sit on during large-group activities. Drew's teacher modified this for Drew by putting his name on his square so that he would be directed to sit at a particular spot in the group.

Samisha sometimes seems distracted by the effort of keeping her balance while sitting in a chair. Samisha has a large block placed under her feet, which helps her maintain her balance so that she can more easily participate in the ongoing activity.

WHEN SHOULD CURRICULUM MODIFICATIONS BE USED?

A modification to the curriculum is the most effective when your observations tell you that the child is interested in the ongoing activities but is not able to fully participate. The child may watch the other children and may try to participate without success, or the child may not stay with the activity long enough to take full advantage. Other children may tell you they are having trouble by becoming frustrated.

TYPES OF CURRICULUM MODIFICATIONS

Table 1 lists eight types of curriculum modifications. The following pages provide numerous examples of each type of modification. Teachers and therapists who work in inclusive early childhood classrooms have sug-

Table 1. Types of curriculum modifications

Modification type	Definition	Strategies
Environmental support	Altering the physical, social, and temporal environment to promote participation, engagement, and learning	Change the physical environment Change the social environment Change the temporal environment
Materials adaptation	Modifying materials so that the child can participate as independently as possible	Have materials or equipment in the optimal position (height, etc.) Stabilize materials Modify the response Make the materials larger or brighter
Simplify the activity	Simplifying a complicated task by breaking it into smaller parts or reducing the number of steps	Break it down Change or reduce the number of steps Finish with success
Use child preferences	If the child is not taking advantage of the available opportunities, identify and integrate the child's preferences	Hold a favorite toy Use a favorite activity Use a favorite person
Special equipment	Special or adaptive devices that allow a child to participate or increase a child's level of participation	Use special equipment to increase access Use special equipment to increase participation
Adult support	An adult intervenes to support the child's participation and learning	Model Join the child's play Use praise and encouragement
Peer support	Utilizing peers to help children learn important objectives	Model Helpers Praise and encouragement
Invisible support	A purposeful arrangement of naturally occuring events within one activity	Sequence turns Sequence activities within a curriculum area

gested the examples of modifications and adaptations. You may be able to think of others that would also work in your classroom. These modifications are organized in two ways. First, the modifications are organized by type. Second, additional modifications are matched to ongoing activities and routines that typically occur in early childhood classrooms (e.g., art center, snack, sensory table).

It is important to remember that a curriculum modification is used to help the child participate. If participation still is not enough and the child isn't learning, try another approach—ELO or CFIS. And remember to evaluate the effectiveness of the curriculum modification. The Evaluation Worksheet is a useful form for this purpose (see also Chapter 3).

COMMON CLASSROOM CHALLENGES

One reason that a child might not participate (or participate successfully) in the ongoing activities and routines of the classroom is that one or more challenging behaviors interfere. At other times, the child may behave in ways that are troublesome to the adults in the classroom. This section covers ways to think about the classroom environment and to modify it as needed in order to provide children with the guidance they need in order to use behaviors that are more appropriate and adaptive in group learning situations.

One of the features of a high-quality preschool classroom is the use of developmentally appropriate techniques that can help children learn appropriate classroom and social behaviors. These techniques are called *structural supports* because they involve careful planning or structuring of the environment, schedules, activities, and transitions with the goal of successful and enjoyable participation and learning in the classroom. Here are several ways to structure the environment for success:

1. Provide a balance between child-directed and adult-directed activities. Provide opportunities for children to make authentic choices.

2. Design a variety of areas in the classroom that are easily viewed and have boundaries. The teacher should be able to view the entire classroom. The children should be able to recognize the boundaries of the learning areas.

3. Make sure that materials are organized and in good working order. Materials should be working and attractive to the children and should be organized in a fashion that tells children where the materials belong.

4. Provide activities that provide many ways to respond. Think about the children's current skills and interests. Plan activities that allow choices and ways to respond.

There are also several ways to structure your classroom schedule for success:

1. Create a clear and consistent schedule. Display the schedule in a way that is appropriate for the children and follow it. Use pictures or photographs as well as words.

2. Use staff schedules. Display and use a schedule for the adults that tells where they should be and what they should do.

You can also structure activities for greater success.

1. Support participation. Use a variety of ways to help children join activities and sustain their participation.

2. Have high expectations. With planning and a positive attitude, you can help all children participate and learn new skills and concepts. Plan interesting and appropriately challenging activities.

3. Be consistent. Children can be most successful and feel trusted and safe when adults provide consistent expectations and are consistent in their responses.

4. Give good, clear directions. Sometimes that means that you must break large or lengthy directions into smaller ones.

5. When children are participating, provide feedback on their performance and efforts. Feedback should be sincere and specific.

Transitions can be the most troublesome part of the day because they are often less structured and more difficult for the child to understand than other classroom events. Here are several suggestions for structuring transitions for success.

1. Teach the expectations during transitions. Be specific in teaching children what to do during transition times.

2. Use pictures or other salient cues. Some children have difficulty with following verbal directions, so add pictures or other cues to illustrate what the child should do during the transition.

3. Begin the activity when a few children are ready. If the activity is interesting and enticing, the other children will join, and those who made the transition quickly do not need to wait.

4. When in doubt, teach the routine. If children are still having difficulty with making a transition, teach them—specifically and systematically—what to do and what you expect during the transition.

Table 2. Ways to address common classroom challenges

Challenge	Environmental support	Materials adaptation	Simplify the activity	Use child preferences	Special equipment	Adult support	Peer support	Invisible support
Child doesn't actively participate at large-group time			x	x				
Child refuses to join large-group time	x			x		x		
Child throws tantrums during large-group time	x		x					
Child talks out of turn during large-group time	x							
Child is not willing to go to or participate in a certain learning center	x			x				
Child has difficulty with making a transition from one area or activity to the next	x			x				
Child is noncompliant when given a direction	x					x		
Child runs in the classroom	x							
Child mouths art materials	x	x				x	x	
Child grabs items from others	x	x						
Child hits others	x	x						
Child doesn't pay attention	x							x
Child whines						x		
Child talks back	x					x		
Child engages in self-stimulatory behavior				x		x		
Child engages in self-injurious behavior	x					x		
Child bites others	x	x						x
Child grabs things from others at small-group time	x							
Child is unstable when walking	x		x		x			
Child has difficulty with descending stairs					x		x	
Child has difficulty with remaining with the group			x	x			x	
Child dawdles	x			x			x	
Child knows an answer or skill but does not demonstrate it						x		
Child refuses to participate in large-group activities			x	x				
Child has difficulty with separating from his or her parent	x							
Child won't remain seated on the bus	x			x				x
Child won't keep his or her seat belt on in the bus	x			x			x	
Child screams on the bus	x							
Child screams in the classroom	x							
Child bullies others						x		
Child doesn't maintain proximity to peers	x							
Child is rejected by peers						x		x

(continued)

49

Table 2. *(continued)*

Challenge	Environmental support	Materials adaptation	Simplify the activity	Use child preferences	Special equipment	Adult support	Peer support	Invisible support
Child falls out of chairs	x				x			
Child has difficulty with sitting at circle time	x				x			
Child bothers others at circle time				x				x
Child has difficulty with beginning and ending projects	x		x	x				
Child has difficulty with washing hands		x						
Child is not yet using verbal communication (speech)		x						
Child runs out of the classroom	x							
Child eats with fingers					x			
Child doesn't respond to transition cue	x							
Child doesn't follow classroom routine	x					x		
Child gives up easily			x	x		x	x	
Child uses toys inappropriately							x	
Child demonstrates low rates of engagement			x	x				
Child has significantly lower skills than the rest of the class			x					x
Child has difficulty with lining up	x							
Child doesn't clean up	x		x	x				
Child is easily overstimulated	x		x					
Child throws up or gags easily and/or often			x					
Child won't come to small-group time				x				
Child mouths inappropriate objects	x					x		

Even when all of the elements of a structural support base are in place, some challenging behaviors may occur. When this happens, consult Table 2, locate the behavior, and find the type of curriculum modification that has a high probability of supporting a positive behavior. Then, you can turn to that section for examples of ways to develop a plan for the child in your classroom. Note that sometimes a curriculum modification is not sufficient. Then, you will need to try an ELO or CFIS. Remember that sometimes children display the challenging behavior because they have not learned a more appropriate or conventional behavior. It's the teacher's responsibility to teach it.

Curriculum Modifications by Type

This part of Chapter 5 provides numerous classroom examples of each type of modification. Each page gives the definition of the modification, the general strategy (i.e., what to do), and examples of when the modification might work. Each page also has space for you to write your own ideas.

Environmental Support

Alter the physical, social, and temporal environment to promote participation, engagement, and learning.

Change the physical environment.

 if   A child pulls things off the toy shelves and then plays in front of the shelves, blocking other children's access…

> …put tape on an area in front of the shelf. Remind children that they must play with the toys outside the taped area.

if   A child has difficulty keeping his or her hands to him- or herself when working on individual activities or projects…

> …provide individual workspaces by using trays, box lids, or placemats.

if   A child has difficulty with putting toys and equipment away…

> …use pictures or symbols on shelves and containers. Make cleaning up a matching game.

Your ideas:

_____

_____

_____

_____

_____

_____

_____

_____

Environmental Support

Alter the physical, social, and temporal environment to promote participation, engagement, and learning.

Change the social environment.

 A child has difficulty playing near other classmates...

...plan cooperative small-group activities with engaging and highly motivating materials so that the child is close to peers while engaging in fun activities such as murals, cooperative block structures, and so forth.

 A child has no play partners...

...build friendships by seating a peer next to the child every day at a planned activity such as small-group or circle time.

 A child is unstable while walking...

...arrange for the child to hold hands with buddies during transitions. With a buddy on one or both sides, the child will be more stable.

Your ideas:

_____

_____

_____

_____

_____

_____

_____

_____

_____

Environmental Support

Alter the physical, social, and temporal environment to promote participation, engagement, and learning.

Change the temporal environment.

 if A child does not participate in learning centers during the free-choice time…

...create a picture schedule for the child. The picture schedule can have pictures or symbols representing the various learning centers organized in a certain order (e.g., art first, dramatic play second, blocks third). The child should be taught to refer to his or her schedule each time he or she finishes an activity or to play in a learning center for a specified amount of time.

if A child has difficulty with making transitions…

...just before a transition, provide the child with a picture or object representing the area or activity that the child should go to next. The child could even take the picture or object to the next area with him or her.

if A child quickly finishes with the snack and then has difficulty with waiting for the next activity…

...open one or two quiet centers (e.g., library, computer) after snack time so that the child can leave the snack table when he or she is finished.

Your ideas:

_____

_____

_____

_____

_____

_____

Materials Adaptation

Modify materials so that the child can participate as independently as possible.

Put the materials at the optimal level for the child.

 if A child has to reach up to the counter to put away the dishes and utensils after snack time...

...place plastic washtubs on child-size chairs or benches for clean-up.

if A child has difficulty with standing, so using the art easel is a problem...

...lower the easel and give the child a chair, or buy or make a tabletop easel.

 if A child's feet don't reach the pedals of the tricycle or Big Wheel...

...tape wooden blocks to the pedals.

Your ideas:

_____

_____

_____

_____

_____

_____

_____

_____

_____

Materials Adaptation

Modify materials so that the child can participate as independently as possible.

Stabilize materials using tape, Velcro, nonskid backing, and so forth.

 A child's arm movements make the art paper slide off the table…

...tape the paper to the table.

 A child has trouble using one hand to hold a toy, and toys (e.g., a jack-in-the-box, hammering toys) fall over when the child tries to use them…

...use clamps or Velcro to attach the toy to a hard surface.

if A child seems to "slip and slide" on the wooden chairs in the classroom…

...attach a section of a bathmat or bathtub appliques to the seat.

Your ideas:

_____

_____

_____

_____

_____

_____

_____

_____

_____

_____

_____

Materials Adaptation

Modify materials so that the child can participate as independently as possible.

If the skill or response required by the toy is too difficult for a child, modify the response.

if   A child has difficulty with turning the pages of a book…

> …glue a small piece of Styrofoam to them; this will separate each page, making it simpler to turn the page.

if   A child doesn't choose the art center because actions such as gluing and pasting are still too difficult…

> …use contact paper or other sticky paper as the backing for collages. Then, the child only has to put things on the paper. (Work on gluing and pasting at other times.)

if   A child has a hard time with grasping markers and paintbrushes…

> …wrap pieces of foam around the markers and paintbrushes to make them easier to hold.

Your ideas:

_____

_____

_____

_____

_____

_____

_____

_____

Materials Adaptation

Modify materials so that the child can participate as
independently as possible.

Make the materials larger or brighter to attract the child's attention or interest.

if A child shows little interest in art activities such as collage or other activities using paper…

…include pieces of Mylar or other shiny paper in the collage box.

if A child shows little interest in the story book during large-group time…

…use a "big book" or use large illustrations painted or drawn by the children.

if A child with visual impairments has difficulty with attending to objects or pictures…

…use pictures and books that are bold and uncluttered.
Use high-contrast colors in visual images.

Your ideas:

_____

_____

_____

_____

_____

_____

_____

_____

_____

Simplify the Activity

Simplify a complicated task by breaking it into smaller parts or
by reducing the number of steps.

Break down the task or activity into smaller, more manageable parts.

if When playing with manipulative toys (e.g., puzzles, beads), a child is easily
distracted by the pieces and often drops, bangs, or scatters the pieces rather than
trying to put the pieces in or on…

...hand the pieces to the child one by one.
Gradually increase the number of pieces the child has at one time.

if A child is overwhelmed by activities such as cooking projects, craft projects, and
table games and is rarely successful…

...break down the activity into several parts. Describe the steps in clear
terms. Draw pictures of the steps to make it even clearer.

if A child has a long walk from the car or bus to the classroom and then dawdles,
complains, and sometimes stops and drops to the floor…

...put photos, posters, or other interesting displays at strategic points along
the way. Encourage the child to go to the next spot; praise him or her.
Then direct the child to the next spot, and so forth.

Your ideas:

_____

_____

_____

_____

_____

_____

_____

Simplify the Activity

Simplify a complicated task by breaking it into smaller parts or
by reducing the number of steps.

Change or reduce the number of required steps.

if The soap dispenser is on the wall and requires that the child reach across the sink and make an upward motion with the hand and because of the distance, the child can barely reach or needs to stand on tiptoes…

...use a plastic bottle with a pump top as a soap dispenser. Place it on the counter or attach it to the sink with a suction cup.

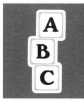

if A child has difficulty with craft projects that have multiple steps…

...prepare the craft activity with individual children in mind. Some children may do the entire project. Others may receive projects that have been started; they do some of the steps.

if A child plays repetitively in the house corner and rarely acts out multiple-step scenes…

...make photographs of three- or four-step play scenes (e.g., put the pot on the stove, stir, and take it to table). Use the photos to help the child lengthen his or her play.

Your ideas:

_____

_____

_____

_____

_____

_____

Simplify the Activity

Simplify a complicated task by breaking it into smaller parts or
by reducing the number of steps.

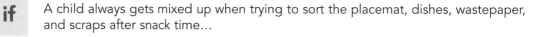

*Break down a complicated task into its parts and
have the child finish with success.*

if A child always gets mixed up when trying to sort the placemat, dishes, wastepaper,
and scraps after snack time…

> *…help the child do each step of the clean-up process until you get to the
> last step. Have the child do this step alone. Gradually increase the number
> of steps that the child does independently.*

if A child has difficulty with washing and drying hands…

> *…help the child do each step until you get to the last step. The child does
> this step alone. Gradually increase the steps the child does independently.*

if A child has difficulty with pedaling the tricycle…

> *…help the child place his or her feet on the pedals and start the rotation.
> Let child finish the rotation (i.e., push down) by him- or herself.*

Your ideas:

_____

_____

_____

_____

_____

_____

_____

_____

Use Child Preferences

If the child is not taking advantage of the available opportunities,
identify and integrate the child's preferences.

Let the child hold a favorite quiet toy.

 A child fusses and tries to leave large-group times such as circle time…

…let the child hold a favorite quiet toy (e.g., teddy bear, Barney). Give the
toy to the child at the beginning of group time.

 A child has difficulty with making a transition from one area or activity to the next…

…allow the child to carry the favorite toy from one activity to the next.

 A child has difficulty with remaining on his or her nap mat during rest time…

…let the child hold a favorite quiet toy or a favorite book.

Your ideas:

_____

_____

_____

_____

_____

_____

_____

_____

_____

Use Child Preferences

If the child is not taking advantage of the available opportunities, identify and integrate the child's preferences.

Incorporate the child's favorite activity or toy into a specific area or activity.

if A child does not come readily to circle time or another large-group activity…

…begin large-group time with a favorite activity such as blowing bubbles or the child's favorite song.

if A child has difficulty with paying attention to books, pictures, or table-top materials…

…incorporate the child's favorite thing into the activity as appropriate. For example, if the child likes dolls, make a lotto game using pictures of dolls from catalogs.

if A child has difficulty with engaging in new activities or learning centers or perseverates on one activity (i.e., does the same action over and over)…

…incorporate the child's favorite toy into the area or activity. For example, if a child loves trains and never goes to the dramatic play area, create a train station in the area, or create a fast food restaurant and use toy trains as the prize that comes with the kid's meal.

Your ideas:

_____

_____

_____

_____

_____

Use Child Preferences

If the child is not taking advantage of the available opportunities,
identify and integrate the child's preferences.

Incorporate the child's favorite person into a specific area or activity.

if A child does not participate in certain learning areas of the classroom. For example, the child rarely, if ever, goes to the library/writing center…

…assign the child's favorite person to this area.

if A child has difficulty with returning to the classroom after the outdoor play time…

…have the child's favorite person tell the child when outdoor play time is over and then walk to the classroom, telling the child that he or she will see the child again in the classroom.

if A child has trouble with staying interested in large-group or circle time…

…have the child's favorite person lead the final circle time activity. Introduce this activity while the child is still paying attention.

Your ideas:

_____

_____

_____

_____

_____

_____

_____

_____

Special Equipment

Use special or adaptive devices that allow a child to participate or increase a child's level of participation. This includes homemade equipment or devices as well as commercially available therapeutic equipment.

Use special equipment to increase access to activities and play areas.

 if The outdoor play area is a long walk from the classroom, and a child who is not yet a skilled walker takes so long to get to the play area that the child doesn't have time to use the playground...

...use a wagon that's big enough for two. Make it a treat to ride in the wagon with the child as well as to pull it. (Make sure the child gets ample practice at walking independently at other times during the day.)

 if A child who uses a wheelchair or walker is not able to get near enough to the sensory table to participate...

...there are a number of possibilities. If the sensory table is strong and sturdy, the child can sit on the table. If the legs on the table can be removed, placing the table on the floor may make it more accessible. Consider giving children individual sensory tables made from plastic bins that can be placed on children's laps, a table, or the floor.

Your ideas:

_____

_____

_____

_____

_____

_____

_____

Special Equipment

Use special or adaptive devices that allow a child to participate or increase a child's level of participation. This includes homemade equipment or devices as well as commercially available therapeutic equipment.

Use special equipment to increase participation.

 A child does not have the hand strength to cut with scissors…

…use loop scissors or other adaptive scissors that require less hand strength.

 A child has poor sitting balance and seems to use all of his or her energy and concentration to sit in the chair with little energy left to play with the toys or color or draw…

…make sure the child has a chair with sides or armrests. If the child's feet don't touch the floor, make a footrest out of a cardboard box or a block.

 A child sits in adaptive chairs or in a wheelchair and during floor activities, the child is not at the other children's level…

…use a beanbag chair or a cube chair in its lowest position so that the child is on the floor with the other children.

Your ideas:

_____

_____

_____

_____

_____

_____

_____

_____

Adult Support

Have an adult intervene in an activity or routine to support the child's participation and learning.

Provide a model of another way to play or a way to expand on the child's play or other behavior.

 A child repeats the same play actions over and over without making any changes, for example, if a child at the sand table dumps and fills and dumps and fills without seeming to pay attention to the effects of his or her actions…

…show the child another way to dump and fill but just make small alterations from the way that the child currently plays. For example, hold the container up high while you dump it, or dump through a funnel or short tube.

 You provide props in the block area that are thematic, but the child does not incorporate them in play…

…take photographs of ways to use the props with the blocks. Place them in the block area and occasionally draw the child's attention to them.

 A child pounds and pokes at the Play-Doh but doesn't use any of the tools…

…take one simple tool like a cylinder block. Demonstrate pounding and poking with it.

Your ideas:

_____

_____

_____

_____

_____

_____

Adult Support

Have an adult intervene in an activity or routine to support the
child's participation and learning.

Join the child's play. By being there, you can show your interest
and provide encouragement by your presence and
through your comments.

 if A child goes to the dramatic play area and watches the other children but does little more than observe…

> …go to the dramatic play area, see what captures the child's attention, and build on that. If it seems to be the hats, then try putting on a hat. If it seems to be the baby dolls, hold a doll out to the child.

 if A child plays eagerly and enthusiastically but is often on the verge of losing control…

> …go to the same play area as this child while his or her play is appropriate. Play in some of the same ways as the child. Try to slow the pace, redirect, or just give a gentle touch before the child's behavior escalates.

if A child is apt to run in the hallway on the way to the playground or bathroom…

> …position yourself near the child. Anticipate. Ask the child to hold your hand or ask the child a question.

Your ideas:

_____

_____

_____

_____

_____

_____

Adult Support

Have an adult intervene in an activity or routine to support the child's participation and learning.

Use praise and encouragement to help the child continue in an activity or routine and to learn from his or her participation.

 A child is taking a book, flipping the pages, and getting another book at the library corner and does this over and over and over and over...

...make a positive comment about the child's play and ask if the child can show you another way to use the book, or you could demonstrate another way and ask the child to do the same action.

 A child usually tries to avoid cleaning up by immediately going to the next activity...

...just as clean-up time is ready to begin, position yourself near this child and start your clean-up song with the child's name.

 A child is not an active participant during singing and other music activities...

...keep a subtle eye on the child. Whenever the child does an action or sings, give the child full eye contact and a smile.

Your ideas:

_____

_____

_____

_____

_____

_____

_____

Peer Support

Utilize peers to help children learn
important objectives.

Have a classmate model a way of participating.

if A child doesn't know how to select an activity or game from the computer menu…

...pair the child with another child who is familiar with operating the
computer, and let the peer show the child how to select an
activity from the computer menu.

if A child is learning how to request food by signing during snack time…

...make sure that the child is sitting at the table with children who know the
signs for snack items.

if A child is watching two children play with a new toy, and the child seems to be
interested in the toy and wants to play with the two children…

...ask these two children to invite the child to join them and show him or
her how to play with the toy.

Your ideas:

_____

_____

_____

_____

_____

_____

_____

_____

_____

Peer Support

Utilize peers to help children learn
important objectives.

Pair the child with another child who can act as a helper.

 if A child doesn't know when and where to line up during the transition to the playground...

...pair the child with another child who knows the routine and follows directions. Ask children to find their partner and hold their partner's hand when lining up.

 if A child has difficulty with lifting and putting the cover back on the sensory table during clean-up...

...ask other children to help. Make it a cooperative project.

if A child has trouble with putting paint on sponges to make sponge prints...

...ask another child at his or her table to put paint on sponges for him or her, and then the child can make prints on the paper.

Your ideas:

_____

_____

_____

_____

_____

_____

_____

_____

Peer Support

Utilize peers to help children learn important objectives.

Have peers use praise and encouragement.

 A child is learning to use words or signs to request food items at snack time…

…have another child hold the requested food (e.g., a plate of orange slices). The child then needs to request the oranges from the friend instead of asking an adult. This can be a nice change of routine: one child has the plate of fruit, another has the basket of crackers, and another has the pitcher of juice so that everyone has to ask a friend.

if A child has difficulty with the table-top toys (e.g., Legos or puzzles or beads) and tends to give up…

…pair the child with a classmate who is fun and talks a lot. Give the pair one set of toys that they need to play with together.

if A child always plays alone on the playground…

…identify a possible playmate who is fun and easygoing. Ask this child to play "follow the leader" with the other child. They can then take turns being the leader.

Your ideas:

_____

_____

_____

_____

_____

_____

Invisible Support

Arrange naturally occurring events within one activity.

Sequence turns to increase the likelihood of the child's participation.

 if A child's hand strength is such that the child has difficulty during cooking activities that involve stirring or scooping…

> …let the child take his or her turn after other children have stirred a bit or after another child has added liquid to the mixture. If the children are scooping out ice cream, let the child take a turn after the ice cream has melted a bit.

if A child is a reluctant talker during group activities…

> …give the child a turn after the turn of another child who is particularly liked or is particularly talkative. This can give the child ideas about what to say or do.

if A child is learning to pour from a pitcher…

> …let other children pour first so that the pitcher is not too full.

Your ideas:

_____

_____

_____

_____

_____

_____

_____

_____

Invisible Support

Arrange naturally occurring events within one activity.

Sequence activities within an activity or learning center.

 if A child needs more practice on a particular gross motor skill such as walking on a balance beam…

...incorporate this skill into an obstacle course. Put a popular, fun, or noisy item after the more difficult one. For example, let the children hit a gong after they walk along the balance beam.

if A child is working on matching…

...during the art activity of making collages, have the child's paper set up for matching; after he or she completes matching the items, he or she can make the collage.

if A child needs practice staying at circle time…

...rotate between active activities (e.g., songs with motions) and more passive activities (e.g., listening to stories) within the circle activity.

Your ideas:

_____

_____

_____

_____

_____

_____

_____

Curriculum Modifications by Activity and Routine

This section provides some additional examples of ways to modify the curriculum to help children participate. These modifications are organized by the learning areas, planned activities, and routines often found in preschool classrooms. If a child in your classroom is having difficulty in a particular area or with a particular routine, find that section and look at the examples. These ideas should help spark your own ideas that will work in your classroom.

The first group of curriculum modifications addresses learning centers:

1. Art center: The art center is an area where children can explore and create. It offers opportunities for children to work and play by themselves, with others, and cooperatively.

2. Block corner: The block area is one of the traditional areas in a preschool classroom. Block building provides opportunities for cognitive development as well as motor development. When props are added, children can extend their play in a variety of ways.

3. Dramatic play: This is the area of the classroom that is intended to highlight children's pretend play. Use materials that are familiar to the children from their homes and neighborhoods.

4. Sensory table: The sensory table provides the children with sensory experiences. They also have opportunities to observe

materials and use tools. There are all sorts of sensory materials, such as sand, water, and leaves.

5. Book corner: The library or book corner is a quiet area of the classroom. It should be an inviting area, and comfortable chairs and pillows help. Books should be displayed for easy access and care. In addition to the books, include a listening center with tapes, flannel boards, and puppets. Some teachers include a writing center or have the writing center adjoin the book corner.

6. Computer center: A computer center increases the number and range of learning opportunities in the preschool classroom. Selection of appropriate computer programs is important. Cooperative play is encouraged when the computer center is arranged for pairs or small groups.

7. Manipulatives: Manipulatives or tabletop toys include a variety of toys such as puzzles, games, and construction materials. They can be played with at a table or on the floor. Such toys offer a variety of learning opportunities and can be used individually or by small groups of children.

The second group of curriculum modifications addresses planned activities:

1. Circle time: Circle time or large-group meeting time is the opportunity for children to come together and develop a sense of belonging. Circle times should allow for lots of child participation rather than waiting and watching. Activities should be meaningful to the children. Adjust the length of time to the developmental skills of the children.

2. Small-group time: Small-group times are often adult-initiated activities that have preplanned learning goals. The same group of children meets with the same adult on a regular basis to explore, investigate, and learn new skills.

3. Cooking: Cooking increases the learning opportunities in the classroom. Children learn about food preparation and nutrition.

4. Outdoors: Children should have time outdoors every day. In addition to physical activity, the outdoor environment can be viewed as an extension of the classroom with both additional and new learning opportunities.

5. Music and movement: Young children learn all sorts of important skills during music and movement activities. Some teachers incorporate music and movement into their circle times, others have a music center available during free-choice times, and others have a scheduled time for music and movement during the day.

A number of routine activities happen every day or several times a day in the preschool classroom. These routines help form the structure of the day. They can also present valuable learning opportunities for children. The routines included in this book are arrival and departure, transitions, clean-up, snacks and meals, self-care routines, and rest time.

Art Center

Environmental Support

Alter the physical, social, or temporal environment to promote participation, engagement, and learning.

A child messes up someone else's artwork or grabs things from a peer…

…provide physical boundaries to the art project by allowing children to do their art in a box lid or on a plastic tray.

A child mouths art materials…

…use big art materials such as big sponges to paint with versus paintbrushes, and put all art materials in a bin with a "no eating" symbol on it.

Materials Adaptation

Modify materials so that the child can participate as independently as possible.

A child has difficulty with maintaining balance at the painting easel…

…cut the legs off of an easel (or shorten them) and place the easel on the table, and the child can sit while painting.

A child has difficulty with grasping a sponge or does not like to get messy…

…glue an empty film canister to the sponge so that the child can grasp the canister instead of the sponge.

A child sucks in instead of blowing out while blowing paint bubbles with a straw…

…cut a small notch out of the straw near the top; this prevents the child from sucking in.

Simplify the Activity

Simplify a complicated task by breaking it into smaller
parts or reducing the number of steps.

 A child is overwhelmed or frustrated with watercolor painting...

*...break down the process into parts. Describe each step in clear,
single-word directions: "Water, paint, paper." Provide
pictures of each step to make it even more clear.*

 A child becomes frustrated with art or craft activities that require many skills
(e.g., cutting, painting, printing name)...

*...partially complete steps so that the child only needs to demonstrate one
skill and then is able to finish successfully. For example, a project requires
children to cut out a house, write their name on it, and paint it.
Provide the child with a precut house with his or her name on it
so that he or she only has to paint it to complete the activity.*

Use Child Preferences

If the child is not taking advantage of the available
opportunities, identify and integrate the child's preferences.

 A child does not play or remain engaged long at the art center...

*...integrate a favorite item, activity, or person into the area. For example, if
the child loves to play with cars and trucks, have some old cars and trucks
at the art center. Let the children drive the cars through the paint and
paint with the vehicles.*

if A child does not choose the art center...

*...pair the child with a preferred peer and let them go to the art
center together.*

Adult Support

Have an adult intervene to support the child's participation and learning.

 if A child is unsure of what to do at the art center…

...an adult can comment on what other children are doing in a manner much like a sportscaster, "Now Jose is dipping his brush into the brown paint, and he is painting large circles on his paper."

if A child repeats the same action over and over again such as pounding the markers on the table…

...the adult can model how to do art another way while building on the child's action. For example, the adult could pound the marker in the shape of a circle, or could pound two spots and draw a line between them.

Peer Support

Utilize peers to help the child learn important objectives.

 if A child is unsure what to do when going to the art area…

...make sure the child goes to the area when other children are there to provide models of ways to use the materials.

 if A child does not maintain proximity to peers…

...plan cooperative art activities with motivating supplies so that the child is highly motivated to use the supplies (e.g., squirter with paint, bubbles tinted with food coloring) but needs to maintain proximity to peers while participating. This increases the opportunities for the child to learn by watching peers model appropriate ways to use the art materials.

Invisible Support

Purposely arrange naturally occurring events within one activity.

if A child is unsure of how to complete or engage in an art activity.

...sequence turns so that another child, who can demonstrate how to start the activity, takes the first turn.

if A child has difficulty with clean-up after art activities...

...limit the number of transitions by having the child go to art just before snack time so that the child only needs to wash his or her hands once.

Your ideas:

_____

_____

_____

_____

_____

_____

_____

_____

_____

_____

_____

_____

Blocks

Environmental Support

Alter the physical, social, and temporal environment to promote participation, engagement, and learning.

  A child spreads blocks across the room…

....establish boundaries to the block area with a rug or brightly colored tape.

  A child is unsure of what to do in the block area or does not progress in block play skills…

…display ideas around the block area such as blueprints of buildings, or photographs of simple block structures.

Materials Adaptation

Modify materials so that the child can participate as independently as possible.

  A child with limited strength has difficulty with the wooden blocks…

…include cardboard blocks. These can be made out of milk cartons and covered with contact paper.

  A child with physical disabilities has trouble sitting on the floor and building…

…put a table in the block area. Let the child stand at the table or sit in an adapted chair at the table.

Use Child Preferences

If the child is not taking advantage of the available opportunities, identify and integrate the child's preferences.

 A child does not play or remain engaged long at the block area...

...integrate a favorite item, activity, or person. For example, if a child loves animals, then place animal props in the block area. If the child likes to pound on things, place workbenches and toy hammers in the block area.

 ## Adult Support

Have an adult intervene to support the child's participation and learning.

 All of the child's building attempts fall down or get scattered, and the child gets frustrated...

...join the child's play. Hand the blocks to the child one at a time to slow the child's pace.

 A child is playing cars and blocks in the block area, repeatedly bangs the blocks together, and makes lots of sounds like car engines...

...take a few blocks to build a road. Place a car on the "road" and imitate noises of car engines while pushing the car along the road. Help the child take more blocks to make the road longer and then push his or her car on the road and imitate the engine's sounds.

 A group of children are playing in the block area, and some of these children get so excited that pushing and throwing can occur...

...then while the children are playing together, join their play, make comments, and make eye contact. This can help prevent some problems.

Peer Support

Utilize peers to help the child learn important objectives.

 A child is trying to build a tower using interlocking blocks, yet can't quite figure out how to fasten these blocks in a locked position, gets frustrated, and starts to throw the blocks…

...ask another child in the same area to show him or her how to put the blocks in a correct position so that they lock together.

 A child moves the blocks around the area but has difficulty building things…

...pair the child with a buddy who likes to build. Encourage the buddy to take turns as the children work on the same building.

Your ideas:

Dramatic Play

Environmental Support

Alter the physical, social, and temporal environment to promote participation.

 A child becomes overstimulated and doesn't engage in play…

> …limit the amount of items in the dramatic play area to only a few things you know the child can be successful with. You can always add more later.

 A child does not engage in sociodramatic play…

> …provide the child with a playscript. A playscript can be developed using either photos or drawings. The idea is to script a two- or three-part play sequence that the child can follow during play. For example, 1) get a pot, 2) put the pot on the stove, and 3) put the pot on the table and say, "Dinner's ready."

 A child perseverates on one play sequence or is disruptive in the dramatic play area…

> …use items from the dramatic play area during circle time and small-group time in order to teach new ways to play. This can provide direction and structure for children who are usually disruptive and can expand a child's play skill repertoire.

Materials Adaptation

Modify materials so that the child can participate as independently as possible.

 A child uses a walker or wheelchair…

> …make sure there is enough space for the child to maneuver. Try it out yourself. You may need two tables in the area so that they are at varied heights.

 A child has difficulty with gripping or handling tools…

> …stock the housekeeping center with easy-to-grip spoons, forks, and handles. Build up handles with foam or tape. Full-size utensils may be easier to hold than child-size utensils.

 A child has difficulty with fastening clothes…

> …make sure the dress-up clothes are easy to put on and take off. Adapt with Velcro. Include items that are simpler to use such as hats, sunglasses, or purses.

Use Child Preferences

If the child is not taking advantage of the available opportunities, identify and integrate the child's preferences.

 A child does not play or remain engaged long at the dramatic play area…

> …develop a prop box that reflects the child's interests. For example, if a child loves trains, create a train station in the dramatic play area with a ticket booth, maps, and cardboard box trains.

 A child does not play or remain engaged long at the dramatic play area…

> …integrate favorite toys, activities, or people. For example, if the child likes the color yellow, place yellow dress-up clothes, yellow dishes, and so forth in the dramatic play area.

Adult Support

Have an adult intervene to support the child's participation and learning.

 A child who is learning language skills plays with a tea set in the dramatic play area, and he or she pretends to pour tea into his or her cup and drinks it…

…bring a doll to the table. Pretend the doll is your guest, serve tea to the doll, and then begin a conversation with the doll.

 A child wanders in and out of the dramatic play area but never gets beyond trying one thing…

…join the child. Watch to see what the child looks at or does. Do the same thing, no matter how simple. Then gradually take turns and expand on the child's play. For example, if the child looks in the mirror, you look in the mirror and say something.

Peer Support

Utilize peers to help the child learn important objectives.

 Children are washing baby dolls in the dramatic play area, and a child wants to wash the doll, but he or she has trouble with taking off the small clothes on the doll…

…ask another child to help him or her take off the baby doll's clothes, so the child can enjoy washing the baby doll.

 A child likes to go to the dramatic play area, but he or she usually seems to be stuck after dressing a doll with clothes and shoes…

…invite more advanced children to play in the area. They can show the child what else his or her doll can wear (e.g., a hat, a purse) and what else he or she can do with the doll (e.g., talk to the doll, walk the doll, have tea with the doll).

 A child doesn't often choose the dramatic play area…

…pair the child with a classmate who likes this area. Ask the classmate to take the child to the dramatic play area for a little while.

Invisible Support

Purposefully arrange naturally occurring events within one activity.

if A child loses interest or always does the same thing in the housekeeping area…

…add props gradually and naturally. For example, add a suitcase to the housekeeping area. Put a few new articles of clothing in it.

if A child loses interest or always does the same thing in the housekeeping area…

…add props gradually and naturally to integrate themes. For example, keep the housekeeping area but add a large refrigerator box that can become a car to go to and from the house.

Your ideas:

_____

_____

_____

_____

_____

_____

_____

_____

_____

_____

_____

Sensory Table

 ## Environmental Support

Alter the physical, social, and temporal environment to promote participation, engagement, and learning.

 A child does not like to get dirty or get his or her hands messy…

…provide child-size gloves that the child can wear while playing in the area.

 A child loses interest or does not engage at the sensory table…

…place novel items on the table each week or hide small toys that children can look for.

 A child always gets wet or dirty during play in the sensory table…

…have smocks on the sensory table so that children can put them on as they enter the area and do not need to leave the area to get a smock and then come back. This can also serve to limit the number of children to an area.

 ## Materials Adaptation

Modify materials so that the child can participate as independently as possible.

A child has difficulty with grasping objects…

…provide easy-to-grasp tools such as shovels, scoops, spoons, or tongs. If necessary, build up the handles with foam and tape.

A child uses a walker or wheelchair and has difficulty with reaching into the table…

…if the table is sturdy and strong, let the child sit in the table. Or put the table on the floor. Or give children individual sensory tables using plastic tubs.

A child has difficulty with seeing the materials…

…make sure the materials (e.g., sand, water) contrast in color with the table and the toys. Use food dye in the water to see if that helps the child.

Use Child Preferences

If the child is not taking advantage of the available opportunities, identify and integrate the child's preferences.

 A child does not play or remain long at the sensory table…

> …integrate a favorite item. For example, if a child loves fish, place water in the table with plastic fish. If a child likes spinning things, place sand toys that have spinning parts on the table.

 A child does not play or remain long at the sensory table…

> …integrate a favorite motor action. For example, if a child loves to pound, place plastic hammers on the sensory table with golf tees and let the child pound "nails" into the sand; or freeze plastic animals in water and then let children pound the ice block with hammers to loosen the animals.

A child does not play or remain long at the sensory table…

> …station a favorite adult or peer at the sensory table.

Peer Support

Utilize peers to help the child learn important objectives.

 A child is pouring sand into a bottle, but he or she keeps tipping over the bottle, gets frustrated, and starts to pour sand onto the floor…

> …have another child stabilize the bottle on the sensory table for him so he or she can successfully pour sand into the bottle without tipping it over.

A child is reluctant to play at the sensory table…

> …pair the child with a classmate. Give the pair a toy to share. For example, give them one bucket and give them each a scoop.

A child does the same actions over and over again at the sensory table…

> …encourage the child to join children who are playful, interactive, and have lots of ideas.

Invisible Support

Purposefully arrange naturally occurring events within one activity.

 A child does the same thing over and over at the sensory table...

...add items gradually and naturally. For example, if the child fills and dumps with the containers, add spoons or shovels.

 A child loses interest in the sensory table...

...place a box or tub of new (or different) toys near the sensory table. Let the children "discover" the new toys.

Your ideas:

_____

_____

_____

_____

_____

_____

_____

_____

_____

_____

_____

_____

_____

_____

Book Corner

Environmental Support

Alter the physical, social, and temporal environment to promote participation, engagement, and learning.

 A child is distracted...

> ...carefully consider the arrangement of your book corner. It should be in an area that is not well traveled and is near other quiet centers.

 A child is active and noisy in this area...

> ....carefully consider the materials that are available. Provide earphones for those who use the tape recorders. Limit the number of children who can use the area at one time.

 A child never uses the area during free-choice time...

> ....use the book corner at other times of the day, as appropriate, to introduce the child to the area. For example, have the child's small group meet in the book corner.

Materials Adaptation

Modify materials so that the child can participate as independently as possible.

 A child has difficulty with sitting on the floor...

> ....provide a child-size table and chair in the area for the child to sit at a table and read.

 A child has difficulty with turning the pages...

> ....place bits of Styrofoam in the upper right hand corner of the pages. It makes them easier to lift. You can also make or use cardboard books.

A child is not yet interested in storybooks…

> ….include photograph albums with pictures of the children. Make photograph albums of field trips and class activities.

Simplify the Activity

Simplify a complicated task by breaking it into smaller parts or reducing the number of steps.

 A child has difficulty with operating the tape or compact disc player…

> ….use green tape (for start) and red tape (for stop) on the buttons to show the steps. Or use numbers for multiple-step operations.

 A child doesn't have the fine motor skills to write but has something to say….

> ….include a magnetic board and letters as another way to express oneself.

Use Child Preferences

If the child is not taking advantage of the available opportunities, identify and integrate the child's preferences.

 A child does not frequent or remain long at the book corner…

> ….integrate a favorite topic into the book selections. For example, if a child loves horses, place several horse books in the book corner. Or if a child has favorite books at home, place copies of these books in the book corner.

 A child does not frequent or remain long at the book corner…

> ….integrate a favorite movement or motor action. For example, if a child loves to make noise, then place some sound-producing books in the book corner.

A child does not frequent or remain long at the book corner...

....place toys that go along with certain books in the book corner.
For example, offer *The Very Hungry Caterpillar* and add some plastic
fruits and vegetables and a caterpillar puppet.
(Socks with eyes on them work great.)

 # Adult Support

Have an adult intervene to support the child's
participation and learning.

 A child rarely chooses the book/library corner...

....station the child's favorite adult in the book corner.

 A child gets very loud or excited when listening to the books on tape...

....have an adult join the child. The adult can use a gentle pat or touch to
help the child control his or her excitement.

 # Peer Support

Utilize peers to help the child learn
important objectives.

 A child flips through the books and quickly leaves the book corner...

....pair the child with a classmate. Have the classmate "read" a story.
Then have them switch.

 A child has difficulty with using and listening to the books on tape...

...hook up two pairs of earphones to the tape recorder. Have pairs of
children listen to the book together.

A child is learning to talk, and he or she chooses to read books during free-choice time...

....let children read stories to each other. The child can have more chances to observe how to tell a story and to practice talking.

Your ideas:

Computer Center

Environmental Support

Alter the physical, social, and temporal environment to promote participation, engagement, and learning.

if A child has difficulty with waiting for a turn...

....have the children sign up on a dry-erase or chalkboard for a turn. After a child finishes, he or she crosses off his or her name. Prewritten names on pieces of paper backed with Velcro can also be used to indicate a child's turn.

if A child wants to play computers when they are not an option...

....indicate that they are closed by covering each monitor with a large cloth or a piece of paper taped to the screen with a stop sign on it.

if A child has difficulty with using the computer center independently...

....provide directions in a picture format posted at the center.

Special Equipment

Use special or adaptive devices that allow a child to participate or increase a child's level of participation.

if Because of a sensory or physical disability, a child is not able to use the hardware in your classroom...

....contact your local or state technology resource center for children and adults with special needs. You may be able to borrow adapted equipment that will work for the child. Look at an adaptive equipment catalog. You may be able to make your own short-term solution.

Peer Support

Utilize peers to help the child learn important objectives.

 if   A child has difficulty with a new computer program...

....pair the child with a classmate who uses slower and more systematic strategies to figure out a new program.

if   A child always chooses the computer and interacts with the computer to the exclusion of peer interaction...

....ensure that buddies use the computer together. Learn the child's favorite program and set up another play area with similar materials.

Your ideas:

_____

_____

_____

_____

_____

_____

_____

_____

_____

_____

_____

Manipulatives

Environmental Support

Alter the physical, social, and temporal environment to promote participation, engagement, and learning.

 A child is easily distracted by the more active centers in the classroom...

...arrange the center to reduce distractions. Use L-shaped shelves. Place the manipulative center in a quiet part of the room.

 A child is always getting into another child's work at this center...

....use trays or box-top lids as individual work spaces.

Materials Adaptation

Modify materials so that the child can participate as independently as possible.

 A child has difficulty with handling the string for bead stringing...

....glue dowels to a board. Use spools or blocks with holes drilled in them as "beads." Place the beads on the dowels.

 A child has difficulty with handling puzzle pieces...

....have a range of puzzle types. Glue spools or small blocks to the tops of puzzle pieces as handles.

A child has difficulty handling game pieces, or game pieces keep scattering during the game...

....use Velcro. Or laminate the game board and pieces and use masking tape to keep things in place.

Simplify the Activity

Simplify a complicated task by breaking it into smaller parts or by reducing the number of steps.

 A child is interested but overwhelmed by the puzzles...

...help the child learn the steps: Spill out the pieces, turn the pieces right side up, start with pieces that form the edge, and so forth.

 A child is interested but overwhelmed by sequencing or patterning activities...

...start the pattern, then let the child finish it.

 ## Adult Support

Have an adult intervene to support the child's participation and learning.

 A child has difficulty with taking a turn or following the rules for table games...

...join the children's play. Take turns with the children and use gentle coaching to help children learn the rules.

if A child insists on selecting the most complex toy, gets frustrated, and throws the materials...

...when you see the child make the selection, join the child's play. Hand pieces one at a time, talk through strategies for doing the activity, or model asking for help.

Your ideas:

_____

_____

_____

_____

Circle Time

Environmental Support

Alter the physical, social, and temporal environment to
promote participation, engagement, and learning.

 A child has difficulty with keeping his or her hands to him- or herself during
circle time…

...provide children with individual boundaries by having
them sit on individual carpet squares.

if A child has difficulty with attending to stories…

...arrange children to be sure that all can see the storybook. Sometimes
children cannot see the book because they are seated too close or too far
away. Select short stories, then gradually increase the length.

if A child has difficulty with attending to rhymes or songs…

....use objects or puppets to act out rhymes or songs to make them more
meaningful. This is especially helpful with students who
speak a language other than English.

Materials Adaptation

Modify materials so that the child can participate as
independently as possible.

if A child is disinterested in circle-time activities and does not yet use verbal language…

...allow the child to make a choice of songs, books, or finger plays by
presenting the choices in picture form. The child can point or select a
certain activity card that is then followed by that activity.

A child does not yet use verbal language and is disruptive or passive during songs and rhymes…

...allow the child to participate by providing him or her with objects or flannel pieces associated with the song or rhyme.

 ## Simplify the Activity

Simplify a complicated task by breaking it into smaller parts or reducing the number of steps.

 A child leaves circle time or is disruptive when stories are read…

...read a story that is repetitive with simple language (e.g., *Brown Bear, Brown Bear, What Do You See?*; *Mapping House*; *Big Green Monster*) every day for the week. The target child will increase engagement because he or she learns the story and can begin to understand it. Other children benefit because stories read repeatedly help children learn to read.

 A child has difficulty with understanding stories…

...use objects or flannel board pieces that represent characters or objects in the story. The child may make connections between the physical object. This can be especially helpful for children whose first language is not English.

 ## Use Child Preferences

If the child is not taking advantage of the available opportunities, identify and integrate the child's preferences.

 A child throws a tantrum and tries to leave large-group times such as circle time…

...let the child hold a favorite quiet toy (e.g., teddy bear, Barney). Give him or her the toy at the beginning of the group.

if A child is not willing to go to or participate during circle time…

> …begin circle time with a favorite activity or toy. For example, when only a few children are at circle time, begin blowing bubbles for them while saying, "Tommy is at circle. He gets bubbles." Other activities include giving children a squirt of lotion, spraying water, playing a favorite movement song, or giving children a turn with a favorite toy such as a whirligig. As soon as the target child arrives at circle time, reinforce him or her with a turn right away.

if A child is hesitant to go to circle time…

> …have a favorite person (child or adult) sit next to an empty carpet square so that the child knows he or she can be near a favorite person as soon as he or she sits at circle time.

Special Equipment

Use special or adaptive devices that allow a child to participate or increase a child's level of participation.

 A child has difficulty with maintaining trunk stability while sitting at circle time…

> …allow the child to sit in a cube chair so that the child is still at the same height as his or her peers, but the sides of the chair provide stability. Once a child's trunk and hips are stabilized, the child can increase his or her active participation because he or she expends more energy moving his or her arms and hands to songs and finger plays and expends less energy sitting.

Adult Support

Have an adult intervene to support the child's
participation and learning.

if A child does not participate in circle-time activities such as movements to songs or
finger plays…

…have an adult sit behind the child and provide hand-over-hand assistance
to prompt the child to do the movements. As the child becomes more
independent, the adult should lessen his or her assistance.

if A child is unsure of what to do during circle-time activities…

…have an adult sit next to the child and model exaggerated movements while
praising and encouraging the child as he or she approximates the movements.

Peer Support

Utilize peers to help the child learn
important objectives.

if A child is asked to choose the picture that shows today's weather and put it on the
weather board but he or she doesn't know which one to pick…

…ask a peer to pick a picture and give it to the child so that the child can
still put the picture on the board.

if Children are asked to choose an animal whose name has the same first letter as theirs
(e.g., elephant for Eric) and pretend to be the elephant during the zoo activity during
circle time, but one child can't think of any animals that he or she can pretend to be…

…ask other children to give suggestions on animals that have the same first
letter as the child's name, and then let the child decide which
animal he or she wants to pretend to be.

if The teacher passes a "magic bag" around during circle time, and each child has a turn
to pick one thing from the bag without looking, but one child just doesn't want to put
his or her hand in the bag…

…ask the child's buddy to pick one thing from the bag for the child.
The child can still hold it while the other children hold theirs.

Invisible Support

Purposefully arrange naturally occurring events within one activity.

 A child often gives nonsensical or inappropriate responses to circle-time questions...

...call on a child who will model an appropriate response just before calling on the target child.

 A child is unsure of what to do at circle time...

...utilize a seating arrangement so that the child is seated between and across from peers who will consistently model appropriate actions.

Your ideas:

_____

_____

_____

_____

_____

_____

_____

_____

_____

_____

_____

_____

_____

_____

Small Group

 ## Environmental Support

Alter the physical, social, and temporal environment to promote participation, engagement, and learning.

 A child grabs objects from others…

…add physical structure to the activity by putting the child's project on a plastic tray or in a cardboard box lid. This way, the child has a reminder of which items are his or hers and are relevant to the project.

 A child has difficulty with transitioning to small-group time…

…assign seats at the small-group table. Post the child's name on the table or on his or her chair. This ensures that children know exactly where they need to sit at small-group time and eliminates transition chaos. Or give child a name card to take to small-group time.

 A child has difficulty with following directions…

…present only one step with corresponding item at a time. Present another step only after he or she has completed the first.

 ## Materials Adaptation

Modify materials so that the child can participate as independently as possible.

 A child is matching word cards to pictures of objects, but the child's arm movements move the cards out of their correct places…

…put Velcro on the back of the cards and the pictures. Let the child attach the cards and the pictures to a board.

 The table is too high for the child…

…attach a foam board or cushion to the seat by using Velcro or tape.

 A child has difficulty with holding a pencil while writing…

…wrap the pencil with tape so that it becomes bigger and easier for the child to hold it.

Simplify the Activity

Simplify a complicated task by breaking it into smaller parts or reducing the number of steps.

 A child has difficulty with puzzles or games that have lots of pieces…

…hand the pieces to the child one by one. Gradually increase the number of the pieces taken out of the completed puzzle.

 A child is overwhelmed by the project the group is working on…

…make picture cards to illustrate the steps or parts of the activity.

Use Child Preferences

If the child is not taking advantage of the available opportunities, identify and integrate the child's preferences.

 A child throws a tantrum and tries to leave the small group…

…let the child hold a favorite, quiet toy or a material that will be used during the activity. Give the child the toy before the activity begins.

 A child is not willing to go to or participate at small group…

…integrate a favorite item into the activity. For example, if a child loves trains, instead of using paintbrushes allow the child to run the toy train through paint to create his or her artwork.

 A child finishes the activity quickly and then wants to leave…

…create "finished boxes" with motivating items inside that the child can only use after he or she finishes small group while remaining at the small group table.

Adult Support

Have an adult intervene to support the child's
participation and learning.

 if A child seems to be confused by the steps involved in a cutting and pasting activity,
and he or she sits there and doesn't know where to start...

...have an adult sit beside the child and show him or her how to cut out a
shape and glue it to the paper without telling him or her directly.

 if A child appears to be getting frustrated in the activity...

....encourage him or her by taking turns with the child.

 # Peer Support

Utilize peers to help children learn
important objectives.

 if A child has difficulty putting the last few pieces of a puzzle in the correct places...

...let another child who has put the puzzle together successfully tell, or give
clues to tell the child where the pieces go.

 if A child has difficulty opening a jar to get Play-Doh or other materials out...

...pair the child with another child so that the partner can hold the bottom of
the container on the table while the child takes off the cover.

 if A child is stringing different shapes of beads during small group, and a child who has
fine motor difficulties becomes frustrated because the beads keep falling out of his or
her hands when he or she tries to hold the string in one hand and hold the bead in the
other hand...

...pair the child with another child, and ask the partner to hold the beads for
him or her, so that the target child can focus on putting the string through
the beads. Or, ask the pair to figure out who will do which part of the task.

Invisible Support

Purposefully arrange naturally occurring events within one activity.

 A child spends most of the time standing or squirming in the chair...

...move the small group to an area of the room where sitting at the table is not required.

 A child has difficulty with understanding the teacher's verbal directions...

...give the child a turn immediately after a child who is successful.

Your ideas:

_____

_____

_____

_____

_____

_____

_____

_____

_____

_____

_____

_____

Cooking

 ## Environmental Support

Alter the physical, social, and temporal environment to promote participation, engagement, and learning.

 A child has difficulty with waiting for a turn…

...do cooking activities during small-group time. Or, do cooking activities on days when you have additional adults in the classroom and break into more than one cooking group.

 A child has difficulty with following verbal directions…

...illustrate the cooking directions by using picture cards.

 A child tends to get into "elbow fights" during cooking…

...place the child at the end of the table, where he or she has more room.

 ## Materials Adaptation

Modify materials so that the child can participate as independently as possible.

 A child has difficulty with stabilizing or holding equipment…

...use nonskid materials on the table. Let the child stand if this helps.

Simplify the Activity

Simplify a complicated task by breaking it down into smaller parts or reducing the number of steps.

if A child has difficulty with using the cooking gadgets...

...have the children work in small groups. Each group contributes to the whole cooking project. For example, one group washes the vegetables, one group peels vegetables, and one group cuts the vegetables. Have this child work in the vegetable-washing group.

if A child has difficulty with doing all the steps...

...set up the cooking activity like an assembly line. The children each do one important step.

Your ideas:

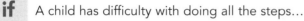

Outdoor Time

Materials Adaptation

Modify materials so that the child can participate as independently as possible.

 A child cannot reach the pedals on the tricycle or Big Wheel…

…build up the pedals with blocks of wood taped to the pedals.

Use Child Preferences

If the child is not taking advantage of the available opportunities, identify and integrate the child's preferences.

 A child doesn't participate…

…don't limit the outdoor space to large-muscle activities.
Add easels and paint; a tape recorder, tapes, and musical instruments; or a
picnic table and board games.

 A child doesn't participate in certain areas of the playground…

…assign a favorite adult to that area.

 A child wants to play ball games but doesn't understand taking turns or other rules…

…teach ball games during the child's small-group time.

Adult Support

Have an adult intervene to support the child's participation and learning.

if A child does the same thing day after day...

...join the child's play, but bring something new with you.

if A child runs excitedly and often gets in the way of the swings and slides...

...make a running track with tape or chalk. Organize a "track meet" or other running event.

Peer Support

Utilize peers to help the child to participate.

if A child is trying to pull a wagon, but it's too heavy for him or her...

...ask another child to help the target child so that together they are able to move the wagon.

if A child has vision problems. He or she has difficulty with going through the obstacle course...

...pair the child with another child who has good vision and gross motor skills. Let the children figure out the best way to do the obstacle course.

if A child is reluctant to try the slide or another piece of equipment...

...ask a classmate to invite the child to join him or her on the equipment.

Music and Movement

Use Child Preferences

If the child is not taking advantage of the available opportunities, identify, and integrate the child's preferences.

 A child doesn't participate...

...incorporate a favorite toy into the activity. For example, if a child likes trucks, have the children roll trucks back and forth in time to the music.

 A child doesn't participate...

...have the children play in groups of two or three. Assign this child to a group that includes a favorite peer or adult.

 A child doesn't do the hand motions in finger plays...

...have the children look at themselves in mirrors while doing the activity. (Use the mirrors from the dress-up area.)

Adult Support

Have an adult intervene to support the child's participation and learning.

A child does not participate actively...

...describe what the child is doing. Introduce new words such as "bouncy" or "smooth."

A child does not try new movements or actions...

...imitate the child. Take turns. Eventually introduce a new movement and see if the child imitates you.

Invisible Support

Purposefully arrange naturally occurring events within one activity.

if A child does not participate during large-group music and movement activities…

…incorporate music and movement into other activities. For example, have the child hop or take "giant steps" to the next activity. Include several of these activities during the day.

if A child is not interested in music activities…

…have the children make their own musical instruments (e.g., drums, maracas, tambourines) during art or small-group time. The child may be more interested in music if he or she gets to play his or her own instrument.

Your ideas:

Arrival and Departure

Environmental Support

Alter the physical, social, and temporal environment to promote participation, engagement, and learning.

 A child struggles or balks when entering the classroom…

> …have the children's name cards or pictures available outside the classroom. Let the child take his or her name/picture card into classroom and place it on a large picture of the school. At end of the day, reverse the process.

 A child has difficulty with getting settled in to the daily routine…

> …place a picture card in the child's cubby. The picture card indicates the child's first task of the day (e.g., going to the block area).

 A child wanders or dawdles on the way to the bus at the end of the day…

> …give the child a picture symbol or a "bus pass" to take to the bus driver.

Simplify the Activity

Simplify a complicated task by breaking it into smaller parts or reducing the number of steps.

 A child acts out while waiting for the other children to get ready to leave…

> …reduce waiting. Arrange for an adult to supervise departure as soon as a few children are ready to leave.

 A child takes an excessive amount of time to complete the various departure tasks…

> …decide which tasks are most important. Have the child do this task or tasks independently. Help with the others. Gradually increase the child's responsibility for all departure tasks.

Use Child Preferences

If the child is not taking advantage of the available opportunities, identify and integrate the child's preferences.

if A child wanders or dawdles at departure time…

…help the child write a short note about his or her favorite activity that day. Have the child carry it home.

if The child's transition from the bus or car to the classroom is slow…

…have outdoor time as the first activity if possible.

Your ideas:

_____

_____

_____

_____

_____

_____

_____

_____

_____

_____

_____

_____

_____

Transitions

 ## Environmental Support

Alter the physical, social, and temporal environment to promote participation, engagement, and learning.

 A child tends to stay in one area and doesn't seem to explore other areas…

…have a timer for the child. When the timer beeps, the child goes to another area so that he or she can have chances to explore all areas.

 A child doesn't seem to know where he or she is going to sit before circle time begins…

…put his or her name on a mat and arrange it before the activity starts. If the child can't identify his or her name yet, give the child another name card and have him or her match the two.

 ## Materials Adaptation

Modify materials so that the child can participate as independently as possible.

 A child has a hard time with following classroom routines. He or she doesn't seem to know what is going to happen in the classroom…

…use a picture schedule. Let the child turn over the card after each activity is finished.

A child continues to have difficulty with following directions during transitions…

…give a silly transition cue. For example, walk sideways to the bathroom.

Use Child Preferences

Incorporate the child's preferences into the activity.

 A child is wandering around in the classroom while other kids are lining up at the door to go to playground…

...let the child's favorite person (a teacher or a peer) tell him or her to come to the line and hold hands while they are waiting or walking to the gym.

 A child has difficulty with making transitions from activity to activity…

...think of a favorite toy or activity the child likes to do, then find or draw a picture of it. Cut the picture into as many pieces as transitions. Each time the child makes a transition, he or she is rewarded with a piece of the puzzle. When the child has all of the pieces, he or she gets to do that activity or play with that toy.

Adult Support

Have an adult intervene to support the child's participation and learning.

 A child doesn't seem to know what to do during the transition from small-group activity to free-choice time…

...close to the end of the small-group activity, tell the child what he or she can do after he or she finishes. For example, you may say, "When you finish that, you can pick an area where you want to go. What areas do you want to play in? We have blocks, books. . . ."

 A child seems surprised or hurried at transitions…

...give the child an individualized warning about 5 minutes before the transition.

 A child doesn't seem to know what to do during a transition…

...listen to your own instructions. Be sure that they are clear, specific, and consistent.

 # Peer Support

Utilize peers to help the child.

 if A child doesn't seem to know what to do and where to go during transitions…

…pair the child with another child who knows the routine well.

if During the transition from circle time to small-group time, children are required to move their photo and name tag from "circle-time board" to "small-group board" at their table, and one child hasn't gotten the concept of moving his or her photo during the transition…

…let some of the other children who know the routine choose which table they want to go to. Have them bring their photos to the "small-group board" before calling on the target child, so the child can see what he or she needs to do several times before he or she actually does it.

if A child doesn't lie down on his or her mat during the transition to rest time and instead wanders around the classroom…

…make sure that other children lie down first before asking the target child to lie on his or her mat.

Your ideas:

_____

_____

_____

_____

_____

_____

_____

_____

Clean-Up

 ## Environmental Support

Alter the physical, social, and temporal environment to promote participation.

 A child becomes confused and distracted during clean-up time…

...outline toys, blocks, and other classroom objects on shelves or place photos on shelves so that this child and others know where toys go.

 A child becomes frustrated during clean-up time…

...use big buckets or bins that are labeled for blocks, toys, and so forth so that the child has a clear idea of where toys belong.

 A child refuses to clean up…

...make clean-up tickets. Draw pictures or use photographs of various areas in the classroom and allow a child to pick a card or ticket. The card he or she picks is where he or she cleans up. When the child is done, he or she gives the card back as a ticket to go to the next activity.

 ## Adult Support

An adult intervenes to support the child's participation.

 A child doesn't know where the big blocks go when cleaning up the block area…

...pick up a few blocks and put them where they belong in the shelves. The child watches and starts to put the big blocks where they belong.

A child wants to help clean up the table after snack time, but he or she doesn't know exactly what to do…

...put a couple of plates in the basket. The child then starts putting other plates and cups in the basket.

A child is trying to wash paint off his or her hands without using soap…

…put paint on your hands, too. Then, put some soap on your hands and rub them together. The child sees it and also puts some soap on his or her own hands.

 ## Peer Support

Let other children help the child complete the task.

 A child is cleaning tables after snack. He or she can't figure out how to squirt soap on the table before wiping it…

…pair the child with another child so that one child can squirt the soap on the table and the other child can wipe the table clean.

 A child often does not wash his or her hands thoroughly after painting…

…pair the child with another child who usually cleans his or her hands well. Ask children to check their partner's hands after washing them.

 A child doesn't help with clean-up time…

…assign two children to a task. For example, one child holds the bin, and another gathers the glasses and puts them in.

Your ideas:

_____

_____

_____

_____

_____

Snacks and Meals

Use Child Preferences

If the child is not taking advantage of the available opportunities, identify and integrate the child's preferences.

 A child eats very little or won't try new things…

...have a favorite adult eat with the children at this child's table.

 A child is learning to use a napkin…

...use napkins that are the child's favorite color or that have pictures of the child's favorite things on them.

 A child eats very little or won't try new things…

...incorporate child participation into snack or meal preparation. This can be something simple like watching cheese melt on toast, making the juice, or stirring the yogurt into the fruit salad.

Peer Support

Utilize peers to help the child learn.

 A child is learning how to use a spoon properly…

...make sure that the child is sitting at the table with other children who can use a spoon appropriately so that the target child can see how others use spoons during snack time.

 A child is learning to use signs to request…

...ask another child who also signs what he or she wants before giving him or her more food so that the target child can have a chance to observe a peer using signs to request.

if A child has difficulty with pouring juice from a pitcher…

...ask another child at the same table to pour juice for him or her. The first child gets to be in charge of another job.

Your ideas:

_____

_____

_____

_____

_____

_____

_____

_____

_____

_____

_____

_____

_____

_____

_____

_____

_____

_____

Self-Care Routines

Environmental Support

Alter the physical, social, and temporal environment to promote participation.

 A child is learning all the steps of toileting or hand washing…

…put pictures next to the toilet or washbasin that illustrate the steps.

 A child forgets to flush the toilet…

…tape brightly colored tape on the handle as a reminder.
Change the tape as needed.

Materials Adaptation

Modify materials so that the child can participate as independently as possible.

 A child can't reach or operate the paper towel dispenser…

…place a basket of single paper towels on the counter.

 A child is learning to zip a jacket…

…enlarge the tab of the zipper by adding a ring or other zipper pull.

 A child is learning to put the correct shoe on each foot…

…place a colored dot on one of the shoes. For example,
use a red dot for the right shoe.

Your ideas:

_____

_____

_____

_____

Rest Time

Use Child Preferences

If the child is not taking advantage of the available opportunities, identify and integrate the child's preferences.

 A child is restless and loud…

...let the child hold a favorite quiet toy (e.g., teddy bear, Barney).

...have quiet books that children really enjoy in a basket that only comes out at rest time. This way even if a child doesn't nap, they can look at "special books" quietly.

...allow a restless child to listen to storybooks or soothing music on tape with headphones, contingent on him or her remaining on the mats.

 A child is not willing to lie down for nap…

...let the child choose where he or she wants to lie down. Offer a choice, such as, "Do you want to sleep on the red mat or the blue mat?"

Adult Support

Have an adult intervene to support the child's participation and learning.

 A child wanders around the classroom…

...go to the rest area. Help children settle down by rubbing backs, talking quietly, or providing books or stuffed animals.

Peer Support

Utilize peers to help the child learn.

if A child doesn't lie down on his or her mat…

…make sure that some children lie down first in the rest area. When the child sees other children lying down quietly in the rest area, he or she may want to do what his or her peers are doing.

if A child is learning how to put his or her things away after rest time…

…pair the child with a peer who knows this routine. Have them help each other.

Your ideas:

_____

_____

_____

_____

_____

_____

_____

_____

_____

_____

_____

_____

_____

Chapter 6

Embedded Learning Opportunities

Early childhood teachers use *embedded learning opportunities (ELOs)* to create short teaching episodes within ongoing classroom activities and routines. The teaching episodes focus on a child's individual learning objectives and are embedded within activities and routines; the instructional component is planned ahead of time.

ELOs can be used when the child shows interest in ongoing classroom activities and when there is a good match between the activity or routine and the child's learning objective. Using ELO has a number of benefits. First, the ongoing activities and routines are used, so this strategy should not require big changes to the classroom. Second, the teacher takes advantage of the child's interests and preferences so this should enhance the child's motivation to participate and learn. Third, because the teaching takes place in the natural setting of the classroom, the child's ability to use the newly learned skill by him- or herself is increased. And fourth, if the teachers plan to provide ELO several times during the day and in different activities, the child's ability to use the skill in a variety of different situations is also encouraged. Bricker, Pretti-Frontczak, and McComas (1998) used the term *activity-based intervention* to describe a total intervention approach. ELO refers to the particular feature of embedding instruction.

One of Samisha's learning objectives focused on increasing her cooperative play skills with peers. One of the ways that Samisha's teachers decided to work on this was to embed planned teaching and learning opportunities within the classroom's free-choice time. There is a learning center in the classroom where the children can play with board games such as Lotto. During free-choice time, Gia and David planned to invite Samisha to the table game center when other children who are more skilled players are there. David then used prompts and encouragement to help Samisha learn the game and play cooperatively with her peers.

In this example, instead of setting up a special or separate time for Samisha to learn and practice cooperative play skills, her teachers did some extra planning so that they could embed the necessary instruction (in this case, using systematic prompting and encouragement) within the ongoing free-choice activities.

THE BASIC STEPS

ELO sounds like the natural thing to do. However, teachers must plan very carefully to ensure that children with disabilities or other special needs get adequate practice. There are seven basic steps.

1. Clarify the learning objective, and determine the criterion.
2. Gather baseline information to determine the child's current level of performance.
3. Use an activity matrix to select activities, learning centers, or classroom routines in which instruction can reasonably be embedded.
4. Design the instructional interaction, and write it on a planning form. You can use an ELO-at-a-Glance, which tells exactly what will happen during a teaching episode (adapted from McCormick & Feeney's "IEP-at-a-Glance" [1995]).
5. Implement the instruction as planned.
6. Keep track of the opportunities.
7. Periodically check to find out if the child has achieved the objective (i.e., met the criterion).

Drew was learning to follow teacher-given instructions. His learning objective stated that during the typical classroom day, Drew would respond to the first request to begin or complete activities. He would respond to at least 80% of first requests and would do so for 2 days in a row. After completing the Child

Assessment Worksheet and examining the daily schedule, Drew's teacher and team decided that they would work on part of this objective during transitions from activity to activity. At this point, Drew's teachers, Jennie and her assistant Marlene, took a couple of days to observe his current performance at following instructions. They made a simple chart with each transition listed and the instructions (e.g., "Time for circle," "Go to small group with Jennie"). They left a place to write "yes" or "no" after each instruction to record whether Drew follows the instruction on the first request. They collected information for 2 days and found out that Drew always needs more than one instruction except when it's time to go outside.

Jennie and Marlene talked about the best way to teach Drew to follow instructions. They decided to use a visual or picture prompt with him because this should help him better understand the direction. Look at Drew's Assessment Worksheet and the Activity Matrix in Chapter 4 to review the planning done by his team (see pages 28–29 and 39–40).

Identifying the opportunities is not enough. Next, Jennie, with help from the team, discussed and wrote a plan for Drew (see Figure 10). This plan, called an ELO-at-a-Glance, tells what will happen during a teaching episode. Good teaching includes 1) careful description of the expected child's behavior (this is the objective), 2) what the teacher or other adult will do before this behavior, and 3) what the teacher or other adult will do after the child's behavior. Drew's ELO-at-a-Glance shows all of these parts. In addition, the form tells the teacher about any materials he or she may need or any changes he or she may need to make to the typical activity in order to embed instruction. For Drew, Jennie needed to have pictures that will tell him what to do next. For example, she or Marlene will show Drew a picture of children at circle time and say, "Drew, it's time for circle." She or Marlene will show Drew a picture of the soap dispenser and say, "Drew, it's time to wash hands."

The ELO-at-a-Glance is paired with the Evaluation Worksheet to collect information to help the teacher determine if the ELO strategy is effective. There are many ways to collect information. (These are described on pages 34–42.)

Information about the child's progress is meaningful only if the teachers have actually embedded the instruction. Sometimes it is necessary to keep track of the adult's behavior to make sure that planned instruction occurs. The space at the bottom of the ELO-at-a-Glance can be used for this purpose. Part of the team's planning should be to decide how many opportunities to provide each day. Once is not enough—try for 10 or more. Teachers simply tally each time they provide an opportunity. Teams should develop data collection forms that work in their classrooms.

Drew's example illustrates how to use an ELO to help a child learn a skill that is best learned within the context of classroom routines. The next example shows how to embed learning opportunities within free-choice time. In many early childhood classrooms, free-choice time or learning center time accounts for a significant portion of the classroom day. Thus,

ELO-at-a-Glance for: _Drew_

Date: _01/07/02_

Team members: _Jennie (teacher)_   _Marlene (assistant)_

Routine: _Transitions_

Objectives: _When shown a picture and given an instruction to start an activity, Drew will_
follow the instruction the first time it is given. He will do this 80% of the time, 2 days in a row.

What are you going to do?   Show Drew the picture.

What are you going to say?   "Drew, go to circle."

How will you respond?   If Drew follows directions, praise and remind him of what he
just did. If not, show the picture, repeat the instruction, and physically prompt him.

What materials will you need?   Pictures or photos of:

Circle time   Each play area   Juice and cookies   Bus
Drew's small group   Soap dispenser   Slide and tricycle

How many opportunities will you provide? (Use Drew's transition chart to track progress)

Monday	Tuesday	Wednesday	Thursday	Friday

Figure 10.   An ELO-at-a-Glance for Drew.

it is prime time for teaching and learning. It's not unusual for a young child with disabilities to have difficulty during free-choice time. Sometimes the child does not have the toy or social play skills that enable him or her to participate during this time. Other times, the child has difficulty with maintaining attention to the activities.

Samisha's learning objective states that during play times, Samisha will join her peers in play and maintain play with them for 10 minutes or more in cooperative play activities. She will demonstrate this in four different play areas. Samisha's teachers, Gia and David, completed the Child Assessment Worksheet, examined the daily schedule, and observed and took notes on Samisha's play during free-choice time (see Figure 11). They noted that Samisha can take part in cooperative play at the dramatic play area but only if she initiates the story line. Even then, her cooperative play lasts only a couple of minutes. Gia and David also noted that Samisha has started to watch other children play games in the table game center.

One of the important considerations for Samisha's teachers is that there are six children with disabilities in this classroom, and many of the children have objectives that could be embedded during free-choice time. Gia and David needed to be creative and realistic about how to use their time and resources. They decided to embed instruction on cooperative play at the table game center. Once Samisha is successful, they'll work on this objective in other play areas. The current plan means that one adult will work with three or four children. The structure of the game and systematic use of prompting will help Samisha learn to play with the other children. They developed an ELO-at-a-Glance for Samisha (see Figure 12).

To maximize their time and resources, Gia and David could decide to use this same activity within free-choice time to embed instruction for another child in the class. Joey is one of Samisha's classmates. He also likes to play at the games table. This could be a prime time for the teacher (who is already there) to embed instruction on one of Joey's objectives. Joey will release a hand-held object onto or into a larger target with either hand. They select the game's playing pieces with Joey in mind and then use slight minimal assistance as needed to help him place the playing piece on the appropriate section of the board game.

TIPS FOR CONSTRUCTING EMBEDDED LEARNING OPPORTUNITIES

Consulting ECSE teachers find the ELO approach and the planning forms useful in their work with community-based teachers. Once a teacher learns the approach and how to use the forms, the approach can be easily transferred to additional children and objectives. However, sometimes the community-based teacher believes that the child needs highly specialized one-to-one time with the consulting teacher. Other times, the IEP is

Child Assessment Worksheet

Date: ___01/17/02___

Teacher's name: ___Gia___ Child's name: ___Samisha___

Classroom activities	Classroom expectations	Child's level of performance
Arrival	Stay with class when walking to classroom. Walk independently.	Strength _____ Average _____ Area of concern __X__
Circle time	Sit on own mat. Participate in music, movement, and other circle activities.	Strength _____ Average __X__ Area of concern _____
Small-group time	Stay at table. Participate in art and other small-group activities.	Strength _____ Average __X__ Area of concern _____
Free-choice time	Play independently. Play with other children.	Strength _____ Average _____ Area of concern __X__

(continued)

134

Figure 11. A Child Assessment Worksheet for Samisha.

Child Assessment Worksheet

Date: __01/17/02__

Teacher's name: __Gia__ Child's name: __Samisha (page 2)__

Classroom activities	Classroom expectations	Child's level of performance
Clean-up time	Clean area promptly when asked.	Strength ____ Average __X__ Area of concern ____
Snack time	Stay at table. Eat snack. Talk with other children and pass items when asked.	Strength ____ Average __X__ Area of concern ____
Outdoor time	Play on equipment in the playground. Play independently and with other children.	Strength ____ Average ____ Area of concern __X__
Transitions	Follow instructions.	Strength ____ Average __X__ Area of concern ____

ELO-at-a-Glance for: _Samisha_

Date: _01/17/02_

Team members: _Gia (teacher)_ _____ _David (assistant)_ _____

_____ _____

Routine: _Free choice: Table game center_

Objectives: _During play times, Samisha will join her peers in play and maintain play with them_ _for 10 minutes or more in cooperative play activities. She will show this in 4 different play areas._

What are you going to do? _Point to or hand to Samisha the game prop (e.g., car, ball)_

What are you going to say? _"Samisha, take a turn" or other appropriate prompt_

How will you respond? _If Samisha follows the instruction, praise and emphasize_ _playing together. If not, hand Samisha the game prop and repeat the instruction._

What materials will you need? _Table games that can be used by two or more children at_ _the same time (e.g., Don't Break the Ice, Lotto, Hungry Hungry Hippo)_

How many opportunities will you provide?

Monday	Tuesday	Wednesday	Thursday	Friday
Free-choice time	Free-choice time	Free-choice time	Free-choice time	Free-choice time

Figure 12. An ELO-at-a-Glance for Samisha.

written in a way that makes it difficult to translate the child's goals and objectives to functional classroom behaviors. Following are some guidelines that may be helpful.

Tailoring the Learning Objective for the Preschool Classroom

It is important to remember that learning objectives are not the same thing as activities. Likewise, planning an activity is not the same as providing instruction (see Giangreco, Dennis, Edelman, & Cloninger, 1994). Community-based teachers are often very good at planning interesting, fun activities for groups of preschoolers; however, in an inclusive classroom, they may not be as experienced at ensuring that an individual child's objective is embedded and that sufficient instruction is provided. For example, a child may have several learning objectives aimed at skills such as reaching, grasping, making a request, or comprehending peoples' names. These objectives are not activities. They are skills that children are expected to use during genuine activities in order to participate more effectively in those activities. The job of the teacher is to teach the child to do those skills and to use them within genuine activities. Just presenting the activities isn't enough; teaching must occur.

Sometimes IEP objectives are written in ways that may actually limit the potential for embedding the objective within genuine classroom activities. For example, one child's IEP objective may state, "Given the cue, 'Put the puzzle together,' when presented with a three- to five-piece interlocking puzzle, Annie will disassemble the pieces and then put the puzzle back together on at least 80% of the response opportunities." This may lead a teacher to implement instruction on the objective by seating the child at a table and providing the child with repeated opportunities with a selected set of puzzles. This is unlikely to occur in an active, play-based classroom, and it may not be very motivating to the child. It's more likely that children will have opportunities to play with a variety of puzzles, various building or manipulative toys, and materials that involve identifying or reproducing designs.

As a member of the child's IEP team, the consulting ECSE teacher can help to write objectives that are functional and generative. An example would be "Annie will assemble toys or objects by putting pieces together. She will do this with at least five different toys available in the classroom such as puzzles, Legos, or stringing beads." This new objective and the teaching procedures go on the ELO-at-Glance.

In preparing to use ELO, the consulting ECSE teacher should work with the team to develop a learning objective or modify the established learning objective so that it can be easily and naturally embedded in many activities (e.g., water play, cooking, art center) and routines (e.g., arrival, snack time, clean-up time). However, if the child needs instruction on a highly specific but necessary objective, ELO may not be the right approach. Here are some helpful hints for writing or tailoring learning objectives:

1. Don't limit the child's initiation of a skill or behavior to just one stimulus/cue. Instead of using the cue, "Child will crawl 4 feet to obtain a toy," try, "Child will crawl a minimum of 4 feet; this may be in response to any of the following: adult presence, peer presence, to obtain objects, to participate in an activity, and so forth."

2. Broadly define the child response, if appropriate. Instead of saying, "Child will request help in obtaining a favorite toy that is out of reach," try, "Child will solve common problems by using more than one strategy such as using a 'tool,' requesting help, reaching around the barrier, and so forth."

3. Avoid limiting the objective to only one material. Instead of saying, "Child will stack three 1-inch cubes," try saying, "Child will stack a variety of small stackable items, including blocks, small books, note pads, cassette tapes, Legos, and so forth."

The purpose is to translate an objective from a child's IEP to a learning objective that can be addressed more easily and effectively in the classroom. The important features of tailoring the objective are 1) teaching can be implemented within routine and planned activities, 2) teaching can be implemented across multiple activities so that the child receives sufficient learning opportunities, and 3) teaching is aimed at the acquisition of new behaviors and skills, not just practice of already acquired skills.

Organizing the Learning Objectives

Identifying or Creating Embedded Learning Opportunities

The child's learning of the objectives is supported by planned teacher behavior. Opportunities are created to perform the behavior and responded to in such a way as to accelerate the child's acquisition of the behavior. One way to do this is to take advantage of a child's interests or preferences (one of the curriculum modifications) when planning for ELO.

One of Nhan's objectives is to increase his vocabulary. Nhan has learned to smile, select a toy or activity, and look busy as a way to avoid talking. However, his teachers also know that Nhan has some definite preferences in terms of toys. He likes to paint, build with blocks, and play ball on the playground. The teachers use the ELO strategy to teach Nhan to say the words. The teachers place these toys on shelves just out of his reach to encourage Nhan to ask for them by name.

Nhan's teacher also places pictures of favorite toys and people and small toys in her pockets. During transition times, she pulls these out to play naming games with Nhan and his classmates.

Creating Multiple Embedded Learning Opportunities

Multiple opportunities to practice targeted skills should be developed within and across activities. Children with special needs often need lots of opportunities to learn a new skill or behavior. An important aspect of making ELO work is to create some new opportunities to make certain that teaching and learning occur.

Designing and Implementing Instruction

Selecting the appropriate teaching strategy can be difficult, but it is so important. The effective use of ELO depends on designing and using good teaching strategies that have a good chance of being effective. Fortunately, research and experience provide information to help make good selections. Some of the things to think about in making selections include:

- Is the teaching strategy likely to be effective?
- Is it normalized? (Is it similar to the approaches used with all children or will it stigmatize the child?)
- Is it useful across environments?
- Is it respectful of the child?

Monitoring the Child's Progress

Collecting data about the use of ELO has two components. First, it is important to keep track of the opportunities that are actually provided. Doing this during the course of a busy and action-packed preschool classroom can be difficult. On the ELO-at-a-Glance, the teacher can make a hash mark each time the opportunity is provided. Some teachers attach a blank piece of paper to the wall and make tally marks there. Other teachers do it differently. In one classroom, the teacher decided that he needed to provide at least 10 opportunities for a child each day. He put 10 paperclips in his pocket. Each time he provided a learning opportunity, he moved a paperclip to his other pocket.

Second, teachers, of course, want to know if the child is making progress. Is the child learning the skill or behavior? Every week or two, the teacher (or the consulting ECSE teacher) should collect child performance data. If the child is making progress, the instruction continues. If the child has achieved the objective, practice opportunities continue, but the team should think about what new objective to teach next. If the child is not making progress, the team should make a change. Thus, the team will have information that is directly related to the child's IEP. Chapter 4 describes several ways to gather information about a child's progress: counts, notes, and products. See pages 34–42 for more thorough discussion of these methods. The method chosen should match the objective, and it should be easy to implement in the classroom. The information is helpful only if it is collected regularly and systematically.

SUMMARY

ELO has great natural appeal to teachers. It is a teaching strategy that uses the typical activities, materials, and routines of the preschool classroom. It should be easy to incorporate a child's preferences and interests. ELO naturally leads to practice that is distributed across various times and events of the classroom.

However, it is important to remember that ELO is a way of providing specialized instruction. It is not just about planning activities. ELO must be carefully planned and carried out frequently enough to result in learning. And it must be matched to a child's individual learning objectives. Children with special needs have difficulty with taking advantage of naturally occurring learning opportunities. Thus, ELO is a specialized strategy that is used to deliver the individualized, deliberate instruction that some children need. The aim is for children to learn their target skills and behaviors and to use them in meaningful ways. Success is measured by the child's progress. If the child is not making progress, even more instructional support is warranted. The next chapter describes what the team can do if the child needs even more specialized assistance.

Chapter

Child-Focused Instructional Strategies

Sometimes, children with special needs require directed, explicit instruction in order to achieve their learning objectives and take advantage of the typical early childhood curriculum. Teachers must use instruction that is more systematic, more frequent, and even more carefully planned than what previous chapters describe. Child-focused instructional strategies (CFIS) are, for the most part, the same strategies that are used in ELO. The difference is the level of intensity. These instructional strategies are techniques and methods for delivering instruction that have been demonstrated to result in improved child outcomes. They help teachers transform opportunities for learning into successful learning interactions (Wolery and Wilbers [1994] provided more information on CFIS). This chapter describes when and how to use these instructional strategies for young children who need specially designed instructional situations, and it defines and describes the strategies.

WHEN TO USE CHILD-FOCUSED INSTRUCTIONAL STRATEGIES

These teaching strategies can be used whenever you want to teach specific skills or concepts. The strategies can be used in a number of different classroom situations and during interactions that are child-initiated or teacher-initiated. CFIS are used when the teacher or the team has identified a learning objective and has determined that in order to learn the objective, the child needs specially designed instructional situations (e.g., Samisha will use her walker or furniture to walk or step from place-to-place in the classroom; Drew will build with the construction materials following the teacher's model).

When using these teaching strategies, remember that all instruction takes place within the context of an interaction. Most often, CFIS occur within the context of an adult–child interaction, but peers can also be effective teachers. Either the child or the adult can begin the interaction, but the adult makes the decision to use this interaction as an instructional opportunity and uses the planned teaching strategy. When thinking about instruction occurring within the context of interactions, it is important to think about the sequence of turns that the different people take. See Table 1 for examples.

These instruction examples are explicit because they are planned by the teacher to help the child achieve his or her learning objective. These same instructions are used regularly, and the teacher evaluates the child's behavior and uses the child's behavior as the basis for changing the teacher's behaviors. The purpose is to facilitate the child's success in learning the objective.

THE BASIC STEPS

The first important step is to decide whether to use specially designed instructional situations or whether to embed the instruction within ongoing activities and routines (ELO) or use a curriculum modification. Some of the criteria that the teacher and the team need to consider follow:

- The child's objective must be unique. Other children in the classroom are not learning this skill or concept. Samisha's objective to learn to use her walker frequently is one example. Learning to use an augmentative and alternative communication system is another example.

- The child must learn a skill or concept to take advantage of or gain access to the general early childhood curriculum. The general early childhood curriculum includes the knowledge, skills, and dispositions that typical children learn during the pre-

Table 1. Instructional interactions

Adult	Child	Adult
"Samisha, walk to the snack table."	Samisha walks with her walker to the snack table.	"All right, Samisha. Have a seat right here." The adult gives Samisha a smile and a pat on the arm.
The adult makes a simple construction with blocks and says, "Drew, make a house like mine."	Drew puts two blocks together.	"Way to build, Drew." The adult gives Drew a point on his point chart and waits for Drew to take the next turn.

school years. It is the foundation for the learning activities that occur in community-based settings such as Head Start, child care, and preschool (Bredekamp & Copple, 1997). Examples of skills or concepts that might need to be taught explicitly to a preschool child to help him or her gain access to the early childhood curriculum are establishing joint attention, imitating children or adults, playing with toys (e.g., Drew's learning to build with blocks), and following simple directions.

- The child must learn a preschool survival skill. That is, the teacher or the team teaches skills that help the child be as independent as possible in the classroom. The primary examples are age-appropriate adaptive skills such as toileting. Other examples include the skills needed to follow the classroom routine.

- The child is making very slow progress despite the teacher's or the team's use of ELO or curriculum modifications.

Once the decision is made to use CFIS, the basic steps are the same as outlined for ELO:

1. Clarify the learning objective and determine the criteria.

2. Gather baseline information to determine the child's current level of performance.

3. Use an activity matrix to select activities or times of the day when the special instruction can be delivered.

4. Design the instructional interaction, and write it on a planning form.

5. Implement the instruction as planned.

6. Collect child performance data daily.

Notice that the final step has changed in intensity. That is, the teacher or the team needs to collect child performance data daily so that he or she can make informed teaching decisions as soon as necessary. Because teacher and child time are valuable resources, the teacher needs to use the resources wisely. Data are collected using one of the methods: counts, notes, or products.

Another way in which the use of CFIS is different from the use of ELO or curriculum modifications is the time that is identified for the specially designed instructional situation. To make this time, the teacher may use a few minutes before or within an ongoing classroom activity.

DEVELOPING CHILD-FOCUSED INSTRUCTIONAL STRATEGIES

Whether the teacher plans to provide instruction embedded within an ongoing activity or routine or as a specially designed part of the day, the basic instructional strategies are the same. The strategies can be divided into three categories: instructions, prompting strategies, and reinforcement strategies.

Instructions

The purpose of instructions is to tell a child what to do. In a classroom, teachers may give some instructions to a single child or to groups of children. An important step in giving good instructions is to know what it is that the teacher wants the child to do. Instructions guide the child to a specific component of a task, activity, or to the materials the teacher wants the child to pay attention to. In general, good instructions are:

- Short
- Clear
- Focused on the observable behavior
- Positive (i.e., they tell the child to do something rather than to stop something)

Table 2 provides examples of instructions.

Prompting Strategies

A *prompt* is something that the teacher does before the child responds in order to increase the probability that the child will respond correctly. Many different kinds of prompting strategies are useful in preschool classrooms but all prompting strategies should 1) help teach skills, 2) be removed as soon as possible (so that the child can do the skill independently), and 3) be combined with reinforcement.

Graduated Guidance

Using graduated guidance, teachers provide the least amount of assistance to a child that is necessary. When help is provided, they should remove the help as soon as the child can do the skill on his or her own.

Table 2.   Examples of good and poor instructions

Good instructions	Poor instructions
"Point to the train."	"I see lots of pretty pictures. Do you see a picture of a train?" (*Note*: the correct answer to this is "yes," not pointing to the picture.)
"Nhan, come play baseball with us."	"Nhan, look, lots of kids are playing baseball. You like baseball, don't you? What would you like to do now?"
To a child who is running around the room during free-choice time: "Drew, do you want to play at the sensory table or with the blocks?"	"Drew, stop running around and think about what you want to do. You need to make a choice."

Samisha is learning to put on her backpack by herself. This involves positioning the pack, putting one arm through the strap, pulling it to her shoulder, and then putting the other arm through the strap and extending her arm so that the strap is on her shoulder. The teacher uses a physical, "hand-over-hand" prompt for the steps of putting on the backpack that Samisha can't do and verbal prompts for the steps that Samisha can do but sometimes forgets. As soon as Samisha learns to do a new step on her own, the teacher no longer prompts that step.

Time Delay

Teachers can reduce and eventually eliminate the prompts they give a child by giving the child a few seconds to do part of the skill before giving a prompt. This prompting strategy, called *time delay,* can be very effective in teaching children to be more spontaneous in requesting and labeling toys, materials, or activities.

Nhan's teacher uses time delay as a way to teach Nhan to use words to request items. At the art table, the teacher holds the art materials, looks expectantly at Nhan, and waits about 5 seconds or until Nhan uses words to request something (e.g., "paintbrush," "paper"). Then the teacher gives him what he asked for. If he does not ask, the teacher reminds him to ask by saying, "Tell me what you want."

Time delay is also an effective prompting strategy for nonverbal responses.

If Samisha always waits for the teacher to start putting the backpack on her, then the teacher could use time delay. The teacher stands near the children's cubbies and says, "Time to get your backpacks on." Then she waits about 3 seconds while looking at Samisha in an expectant way. If Samisha begins the task, the teacher smiles and helps as needed. If Samisha waits, the teacher could give a more direct instruction such as "Samisha, put your backpack on," and wait another 3 seconds.

Backward Chaining

For some objectives, it may make more sense for the teacher to provide prompts or assistance for the entire sequence of steps at first.

Tina's teachers, Dolores and Maggie, use backward chaining to help Tina learn to fasten her clothing. At first, Dolores or Maggie would use hand-over-hand assistance to get the fasteners lined up and to apply some pressure. Then, they started to remove their assistance at the last step (e.g., snapping the snaps, finishing the zip). Then, they started to remove their assistance at the step of applying pressure. For the last step, they will remove their help at lining up the fasteners, and Tina will be able to do the whole series of steps by herself. While she's learning this series of steps, Tina experiences success at the completion of the task of fastening.

Reinforcement Strategies

Research and experience provide evidence to support the use of reinforcement procedures to help children learn. *Reinforcers* are things (e.g., words, activities) that follow a behavior. Instructions are prompts that occur before the child's behavior; reinforcers are what teachers do immediately after the child's behavior or response. Our focus is on the use of positive reinforcement.

Positive Reinforcement

In technical terms, *positive reinforcement* is something that follows a specific response and increases the likelihood that the response will happen again. Reinforcement is used extensively in educational environments and can be very simple and natural. For example, after a child asks for a ball, the teacher gives him or her the toy and says something like, "Here you go. Here's the ball." It may be more systematic and formal: After Tina gets her clothes fastened, the teacher says, "Wow, Tina, you snapped your snaps!" and puts a star on her chart. Positive reinforcement is usually a pleasant consequence; it has the high probability of increasing whatever behavior preceded it.

An important feature of positive reinforcement is that what functions as a reinforcer is very specific to each child and varies over time. Although teacher praise, encouragement, and smiles may be powerful reinforcers for most preschool children, you cannot assume that these will be effective for all children. The only way to determine if something is a reinforcer is to examine the effect it has on a child's behavior.

Differential Reinforcement of Other Behavior

The idea behind *differential reinforcement of other behavior (DRO)* is to catch the child being good, and let him or her know it! This technique is used when you want to decrease a challenging behavior in the classroom by providing the child with positive reinforcement for behaviors that are incompatible with the challenging behavior. For example, if a child is very active and moves rapidly from one activity to another without really playing at any activity, you could use a DRO procedure to provide feedback for the child when he or she does stay at an activity and becomes engaged in play.

Peer-Mediated Strategies

Teachers cannot be everywhere at once, so in some inclusive preschools, the teacher can rely on peers to assist children with special needs in learning or practicing some skills. To incorporate peers into an individualized program for a child with special needs, several points are important.

- The peer needs to know how to do the skill. For example, if the objective for the child with special needs is to follow the routine of going outside, the peers who are helping should be able to do each step of going outside by themselves.

- The peers need to know what to do to help the child with special needs learn the skill. The teacher must explain to the peers exactly what they should do in helping the child with special needs. For example, the teacher goes over each step of the routine with the peers. Peers should only provide help when the child cannot do a part of the task. For example, the child with special needs may be able to find his or her cubby when the teacher says, "Time to line up and go outside," but when the child is at the cubby, he or she cannot put on his or her jacket all the way. The peers need to know to not help when the child is finding his or her cubby but to provide help with the jacket.

- Different peers should be incorporated into the learning process. The teacher should choose several peers to be helpers for the child with special needs. One peer who is asked to be a helper all of the time may grow tired of it.

- The peers need to know that the teacher values their work. Teachers can show how much they value the peers' assistance in several ways. They can praise them, give them a hug or pat, or provide a more formal reward such as getting to do a special activity. Such adult recognition is a critical part of most peer-mediated teaching approaches.

- The peers should be taught not to treat the child with special needs as the "helpee." The teacher should point out the ways that the child with special needs can do some things independently (i.e., recognize his or her strengths). If fact, sometimes it's

147

appropriate to ask a child with special needs to be the peer helper. Also, when peers are giving too much assistance or assisting with things the child already knows how to do, the teacher needs to step in and suggest that they wait to see whether the child can do the task by him- or herself.

- Remember that some of the curriculum modifications also involve peers but may require less time teaching the peers. Examples are the ways that teachers group children for some activities, using peer buddies, and other simple modifications.

The examples in this chapter should guide teachers and their teams in the use of more explicit instruction. The forms in Chapter 4 provide direction for planning. The teacher may want to use the ELO-at-a-Glance to guide the instructional episodes. The critical differences are that the teacher needs to be very clear about each instructional step, and the teacher collects child performance data every day.

TIPS FOR USING CHILD-FOCUSED INSTRUCTIONAL STRATEGIES

You should consider a number of issues when using CFIS and implementing the strategies described in this chapter. Additional resources to consult for using CFIS are found in Appendix B.

Scheduling

It may seem overwhelming to try to identify times during a busy day when the teacher or other adult can concentrate on a single child and provide specialized instruction. However, it's likely that this child is already demanding your attention. For example, this may be the child you always have to help, remind, or have by your side. Why not use the time more productively? Here are some ideas:

- Identify and use times when the other children are independent and engaged in activities. This might be in the middle of free-choice time, out on the playground, or at snack time.

- Select times that are followed by a fun or preferred activity. The specially designed instructional time is hard work; make sure it is followed by something fun.

- Don't select times that are the child's favorite or times when the child is successful in the classroom. No one wants to leave something he or she enjoys or is good at.

- Even a few minutes of special time is worth it. Be consistent and provide this time every day.

Selecting Materials

Here are some things to keep in mind when selecting the materials to use to help the child learn his or her specific learning objective.

- Use materials that are similar to what the child uses in the classroom or community.
- Use materials that are developmentally appropriate.
- Vary the materials.
- Use materials that are appropriate to the learning objective and are preferred by the child.

Motivation

Not many people are motivated to work on something that's difficult without some added incentive. Here are some ideas for making CFIS time more enjoyable:

- Identify potential motivators. These can be activities such as playground time, listening to music, or rocking in a rocking chair. There are also tangible motivators such as a favorite toy or a sticker. There are also social motivators such as a smile and a pat on the back. Give the child choices from a set of potential motivators. Keep track of those the child prefers.
- During the teaching time, use a motivator along with the positive feedback you give to the child.
- Make sure that the child keeps getting these motivators at a rate that keeps the child trying. For example, if a child likes to make paper chains, give the child a slip of paper for every correct response. When the child gets 10 (or at the end of the session), let the child make the paper chains.
- If special time involves more than one child, make sure that the activity is motivating for everyone.

Monitoring Progress

It is important to collect regular data on the child's performance so that the teacher or the team can decide whether to continue the instruction or to change it. It's unfair to the child to continue doing the same thing if the child is not learning. The consulting ECSE teacher should devise a way of collecting these data so that the ECE teacher or assistants can carry out the plan, given the time and resources available to them. It may be the consulting ECSE teacher's responsibility to do a check or "mini-test" every few days to make sure that the child is learning the skill or concept.

SUMMARY

This chapter describes how and when teachers and teams use more explicit CFIS. The strategies themselves (i.e., using good instructions, prompting, and reinforcement) are the same strategies used for ELO. The difference is the intensity with which instruction is provided. Sometimes, children continue to have difficulty with learning despite rich and inviting activities and environments and despite teachers' attempts to provide additional learning opportunities. Some children have very individual learning needs that demand more explicit instruction. In any case, it is the team's responsibility to ensure that sufficient and appropriate teaching occurs.

Four
Important Topics

Chapter 8

Independent Classroom Behavior

he first seven chapters of this book describe practices that can be used in a variety of early childhood classrooms. The last four chapters demonstrate how to apply the Building Blocks framework in four important content areas. Why discuss these curriculum content areas? According to child development literature, many important developmental tasks are accomplished during the early childhood years. Furthermore, certain content areas are becoming increasingly vital to ECE teachers. Through observations of early childhood classrooms and conversations with many teachers, four crucial content areas have been identified:

1. Independent classroom behavior

2. Developmentally appropriate classroom behavior

3. Emergent literacy in the early childhood classroom

4. Friendships and relationships

These curriculum content areas may be particularly problematic for children with disabilities and other special needs.

Tina attends Head Start at the community center in her neighborhood. Her teachers and her mother are pleased with her progress. She participates in the classroom activities and plays with the other children in the classroom. She has learned many new skills and concepts this year. As part of her kindergarten

transition plan, the consulting ECSE teacher, Tamika, observed Tina in her class-
room. Tamika was concerned by Tina's lack of independence in the classroom. She
observed that a teacher or another child was always available to help Tina through
transitions, completing tasks, and managing her materials. Tamika wondered what
the team could do to help Tina learn some independence skills that will help her
succeed in kindergarten.

Independence includes being able to rely on oneself and one's own ability, being self-confident, and being self-reliant. These valued characteristics appear to be related to school and work success. Although it is premature to talk about vocational choices when children are in preschool, some of the foundational skills and behaviors taught in preschool serve children throughout their lifetimes. Independence skills are foremost among these important and functional skills. Independent classroom behavior in preschool includes but is not limited to:

- Making independent transitions within the classroom and school (e.g., walking from the classroom to the playground without holding the teacher's hand)

- Managing personal possessions and classroom materials appropriately (e.g., hanging up coat and backpack in cubby)

- Completing developmentally appropriate tasks without adult assistance

- Staying engaged in an appropriate play activity

- Actively participating in a developmentally appropriate group activity

- Appropriately completing of self-care tasks such as toileting, dressing, eating, and nose care

The ability to stick to a task and complete it independently is highly valued by kindergarten and elementary school teachers, yet these skills are often not explicitly taught in preschool classrooms. In fact, children's opportunities to be independent or to practice doing things by themselves are often preempted. This chapter suggests strategies that can be used in inclusive preschool classrooms to help children develop and practice appropriate independent behavior. (To read more about helping children become more independent, see Allen & Schwartz, 2001; Azrin & Foxx 1989; and Baker, 1997.)

TEACHING INDEPENDENCE SKILLS

One of the first steps in teaching children to be more independent is to determine what skills to target. It is very important to remember that children cannot and should not be expected to complete a skill or behavior independently until they can complete it accurately and fluently with adult supervision. Once children have shown mastery of skills, it is time to consider helping them become more independent with those skills. Therefore, independent performance can be thought of as another level of skill acquisition; teachers can begin to plan for independence in the same way they plan for generalization and maintenance.

Next, you need to determine when you are going to teach independence. Like any new skill, independence must be taught. This includes providing multiple opportunities across the day to be independent and systematically decreasing the amount of support the child receives while maintaining appropriate child behavior. The steps outlined in Chapter 4 may help the teacher or the team to identify the child's learning needs and to plan how to teach the identified skills.

Once the team has decided what skill to target for independence, the team needs to assess how much support the child is currently receiving to complete the task. When teaching independence, select tasks that have steps the child can complete independently. For example, if a teacher wants to address hanging up the child's coat and backpack on arrival in the classroom, the teacher needs to be sure that the child can complete all the steps of that task. Then, the teacher needs to determine how much teacher and peer support is currently provided to complete the task. For example, can the child do it if a teacher is standing right next to him or her? Does the teacher need to talk the child through the task and provide constant encouragement to keep going?

When describing the amount of support a child currently receives, consider two categories of support: physical support and instructional support. *Physical support* includes proximity, any touching of the child (e.g., holding his or her hand during transitions), and physically helping a child complete a step of the task (e.g., turning on the water during hand washing). *Instructional support* includes teacher directions, comments, praise, and encouragement. Understanding the amount of support that children currently receive helps teachers determine what tasks are good candidates for independence training and helps them determine how to change their own behaviors to facilitate independent child responses.

The next step is to determine when to teach the identified skills. Using the activity matrix, the team can plan times of the day when all of the children will work on independent tasks or schedule times to provide special instruction on target skills for individual children. For some teachers, one of the most difficult parts of teaching independence skills is providing children with opportunities to be independent. It is easy to fall into habits of offering help. Teachers who have this habit can schedule their own activities within the activity matrix. If a child can already put his or her things in the cubby but always waits for help, then the teacher can schedule him- or herself to welcome the child at the first activity of the day rather than while standing at the cubbies. If the child needs instruction in the steps involved in becoming independent, the teacher can schedule him- or herself to be nearby.

The next step is to begin the independence training. When planning the intervention, consider what you expect the child to do and what you do while the child is working independently. Do you need to prepare any special materials or organize materials in a particular way to facilitate child independence? Remember that as you decrease the amount of support you provide the child, you still need to provide praise and encouragement. In planning this part of the intervention, it may be helpful to spend a day observing a classroom that is the next environment or the next age group (e.g., kindergarten) to see the level of independence demonstrated by the children in the classroom. It is most helpful to try to observe early in the year to get an idea of what children are doing at the beginning of the school year.

It is also important to remember that cultural traditions and beliefs about children influence notions about developmentally appropriate independence. For example, the norms for independent eating vary from one culture to another. Teachers and their team members should learn about the beliefs of families in their programs as well about their own beliefs regarding independence.

Finally, in order to teach independence to children, you need to provide children with multiple opportunities throughout the day across different activities to be independent. Begin with small steps. If you are teaching children to walk in the halls without holding the teacher's hand, it does not mean that you can never hold a child's hand; rather, it means that you do not need to hold the child's hand. You can also begin to teach children to complete work independently early in preschool. When children are working on tabletop activities (e.g., puzzles, manipulatives, visual discrimination tasks such as matching parquetry blocks), allow them to complete the activity independently. Often, in the attempt to be helpful, adults preempt children's opportunities to develop the ability to do things by themselves. Children need these opportunities to develop self-reliance and self-confidence. So, perhaps the most important part of teaching independent classroom behavior is to provide opportunities for children to be independent and support their accomplishments.

Tina's teachers asked the consulting ECSE teacher to help them pinpoint Tina's learning needs in the area of independence. Together they decided to begin working on greater independence at the learning centers using ELOs. Their observations told them that while Tina's picture schedule helped her move from activity to activity, she was often slow to begin the transition. Consequently, a peer was often asked to hold her hand to get her to the next activity. The teachers planned a new intervention that they used for all the children. Everyone was told to make the transition "all by yourself" and a highly pre-

ferred event followed for those who got to the next activity all by themselves. Tina received a selected reinforcer if she was one of the first to make the transition. After a week, the new plan appeared to be working.

Table 1 provides additional examples of instructional support at each level of the Building Blocks framework.

SUMMARY

Independence doesn't appear as a separate domain in most early childhood curricula. Yet, independent behavior is implicit in many aspects of

Table 1. Tips for supporting independent classroom behavior

Child-focused instructional strategies (CFIS)	Teach children the play skills needed to participate in classroom activities
	Teach children the self-help skills needed to perform and participate in routine events; gradually decrease the adult's support to encourage independence
	Teach children the steps involved in completing classroom routines such as putting materials in their cubby, getting ready to go outside or come back inside, getting ready for snack time, or cleaning up after play time; gradually decrease the adult's support to encourage independence
Embedded learning opportunities (ELO)	Provide opportunities for children to practice the steps in classroom routines
	Incorporate independence skills within relevant classroom themes or projects (e.g., practice brushing teeth to a special song, do a project on shoes to offer practice putting on shoes)
	Add a "finished box" for appropriate activities (e.g., when children are finished writing in their journals, they can put the journal in the finished box)
Curriculum modifications (CM)	Use process charts for hand washing and other tasks to help children remember all the steps
	Place materials at the children's level so that they can get them by themselves
	Allow extra time for children to complete a task without adult assistance
	Use pictures or objects to help children remember where they are going during a transition
	Use pictures, labels, or special containers to help children be more independent during clean-up time
	Use preferred materials and rotate materials in the learning centers to help encourage engagement
High-quality early childhood environment	Have developmentally and chronologically age-appropriate expectations for all children
	Provide opportunities to experiment with new tasks, materials, and activities
	Include opportunities for children to do things independently and have adults available when the child requests assistance
	Provide a predictable schedule, routines, and staff
	Provide facilities and equipment that are the appropriate size for young children

the curriculum. It refers to managing one's personal needs and adapting one's behaviors to the social expectations of the teachers and the other children in the group. Learning these sorts of skills is often a factor in a child's successful participation in community-based classrooms and other activities.

All young children are learning to be more independent. For example, their teachers help them learn to put on their shoes and coats, follow classroom routines, and persist in solving problems. Children with disabilities or other special needs may need modifications to the materials or the skill, extra practice, or more deliberate teaching in order to learn independence. This chapter reminds teachers to evaluate their own behaviors so that they don't provide too much help. The Building Blocks framework can guide teachers in selecting and using the right amount of help.

Chapter

9

Developmentally Appropriate Classroom Behavior

Grace Martin started off the school year with high hopes. Over the summer, she worked on her teaching certificate and participated in a week-long workshop on promoting appropriate classroom behavior at a local university. The course made sense to her, although classroom management (as she always thought of it) had never been her strength. However, now it is November, and she is frustrated; the strategies they talked about in her workshop seem impossible to implement in her classroom, and she feels like she is spending too much time disciplining and not enough time teaching. She does not know where to start or who to turn to for help.

Drew, who has autism, enjoys school—once he is there. He seems to enjoy every activity at school once he is engaged in the activity. In fact, he does not like to stop any activity in which he is engaged either at home, school, or child care. When he is asked to stop one activity and move to another, he usually begins to have a tantrum. Often, teachers and his parents let him continue doing what he is doing, but when they require him to move onto the next activity, he often cries during the entire transition. Once he is settled at the

new activity, he calms down and begins to participate in an appropriate manner. Drew's transition behavior is stressful for the children and adults in the classroom, and many children are beginning to avoid Drew because of this behavior. His parents also report that this behavior is becoming more difficult to deal with at home and in the community. What strategies can help Drew, his parents, and his teachers to have more successful transitions?

Most young children, both with and without disabilities, demonstrate some challenging or inappropriate behavior at times. Experimentation with rules, boundaries, and consequences is a normal part of child development. For some young children, however, learning how to use materials appropriately and how to interact with peers and adults in group settings can be very challenging. It is essential that children learn these developmentally appropriate classroom behaviors because they affect success in early childhood settings and in subsequent educational and community settings.

This chapter provides some practical suggestions for teachers to use to support appropriate classroom behavior and to decrease challenging behaviors that interfere with children's participation in classroom and community settings (see Table 1). Testing limits and asserting one's independence are part of growing up; this chapter does not address the types of limit-testing behavior that is typical of young children. Rather, these are strategies that can be applied at a classroom level to prevent challenging behaviors and with individual children when a challenging behavior persists (Sandall & Ostrosky, 1999).

This chapter uses the term *challenging behavior* to refer to behavior that is persistent; that interferes with a child's participation in classroom, community, or home activities; and that is perceived by parents and teachers to be a problem. These strategies are based on many years of work with young children and the burgeoning research literature on positive behavioral support.

POSITIVE BEHAVIORAL SUPPORT

Positive behavioral support (PBS) is a comprehensive approach focusing on facilitating appropriate behaviors while preventing and reducing challenging and stigmatizing behaviors. A major goal of PBS is to facilitate participation in meaningful activities and inclusive settings. A fundamental tenet of PBS is that challenging behaviors have a communicative function. In other words, when children demonstrate these behaviors, they are trying to communicate something. They may be asking for attention or asking to be left alone; they may be trying to obtain some materials or trying to tell someone else that they do not want to share the materials.

Table 1. Tips for supporting developmentally appropriate classroom behavior

Child-focused instructional strategies (CFIS)	For children who do not have an effective communication system, teach children to request and to make an appropriate form of protest
	Teach children specific vocabulary to use in problem solving
	Teach children to label emotional states and be able to provide positive solutions to potential problems
	If a child is aggressive toward peers and the result of the functional behavior assessment (FBA) suggests he or she is attempting to gain their attention, teach the child a more appropriate way to get their attention (e.g., tapping the person on the shoulder)
	Teach children to use a solution chart, a visual support strategy that suggests alternative ways to solve problems
Embedded learning opportunities (ELO)	Use individual picture schedules and timers to help children stay engaged in center activities for a specified length of time
	Systematically teach children how to request toys from peers to decrease grabbing and aggression
	Systematically teach children problem-solving skills for times when peer conflicts can occur
	Teach children to use words to label their emotional states when they are experiencing the emotion (e.g., happy, sad, mad, frustrated)
	Provide a great deal of positive feedback for children who come to the planned activity
Curriculum modifications (CM)	Assign seating for small-group activities and class meetings
	Use picture schedules and other visual support strategies, including process charts that outline complex play activities
	Use work mats and other strategies to help children define their own space
	Limit the number of children in a center at one time to avoid crowding
	Provide activities and materials in every center that appeal to the interest and abilities of the entire range of children in your classroom
High-quality early childhood environment	Provide a clear and consistent classroom schedule
	Use a few simple classroom rules
	Offer a well-designed environment including clearly marked activity centers
	Provide interesting, developmentally appropriate and well-maintained materials
	Include a variety and balance of activities, including activities for both active and quiet play

The idea that challenging behaviors have a communicative function changes the approach to managing these behaviors. Rather than attempting to eliminate the behaviors immediately, teachers should understand what the child is attempting to communicate and then teach the child a more appropriate way to accomplish his or her goal. This shifts the emphasis from adult-directed classroom management systems to more shared control between adult and child with an emphasis on supporting the child's appropriate behavior while making sure that the inappropriate behavior is no longer effective in achieving the communicative goal.

WHAT ARE DEVELOPMENTALLY APPROPRIATE CLASSROOM BEHAVIORS?

Developmentally appropriate classroom behaviors include the basic skills that most preschool children can demonstrate. This includes but is not limited to

- Following simple directions given to an individual
- Following simple directions given to the group
- Making classroom transitions, including putting materials away
- Following basic classroom rules
- Regulating and expressing emotions in an appropriate manner
- Using appropriate and peaceful strategies to resolve conflicts with peers
- Stopping an inappropriate behavior when asked by an adult

When addressing challenging behaviors, it is always important to begin by identifying the appropriate alternative behavior. Whenever trying to decrease or eliminate a child's challenging behavior, the teacher needs to consider what function the behavior serves for the child and how well that child will be able to achieve that function in a more appropriate manner. For example, Drew's behavior during transitions may mean that he does not understand why he needs to stop one activity, and he doesn't know what the next activity will be. Drew's teachers and family could help Drew achieve this need for information by providing him with visual cues (e.g., pictures or symbols) for the transition.

A common and often very upsetting challenging behavior in preschool is aggression. Aggression includes hitting, kicking, pinching, throwing objects at people, and other types of unfriendly touching. Aggression is sometimes difficult for staff members to deal with because most people bring with them preconceived, and often very strong, beliefs about how to deal with aggression in young children. Using a PBS approach requires that teachers disregard their preconceived notions and address aggression systematically. Coping with children's aggression is a formidable task, especially when children are aggressive toward their peers, because school must be a safe place for *all* children. As one preschool administrator tells parents in her center when asked about a child who demonstrates aggressive or dangerous behavior, "The behavior is unacceptable and must be eliminated, but the child is a member of our school and it is our job to teach him some more appropriate alternatives." The next section discusses how to teach appropriate behaviors that can take the place of those challenging behaviors.

TEACHING DEVELOPMENTALLY APPROPRIATE CLASSROOM BEHAVIOR

The Building Blocks model, described throughout this book, is an appropriate way to approach challenging behaviors. What is important about this approach is that it is not a "one size fits all" way to deal with behavior. It also encourages teachers to work with the team, including the family, to provide the right amount of support and instruction to the child (Melloy, Davis, Wehby, Murry, & Leiber, 1998). When dealing with challenging behaviors, teachers should begin by looking at what exists in the classroom (see the *Quality Classroom Assessment Form*). The classroom must provide appropriate activities, including a mix of active and quiet activities; an appropriate environment, including enough space and materials in good working order; and an appropriate level of structure, including a schedule, simple classroom rules, and a room with clearly defined centers.

Some children may need modifications to the physical or temporal environment and to the activities in the classroom. Many children, such as those who have difficulty with receptive language, may benefit from picture schedules or other visual cues, which help to decrease challenging behaviors during transitions and free-choice time. Other children may need other visual reminders to help them participate more fully, such as work mats during art projects, carpet squares during circle time, or labels on containers to facilitate clean up. Other children may need more explicit instruction to acquire more appropriate alternate behaviors. For example, Drew needs explicit instruction to learn how to use the picture schedule and other visual supports, but once he learns the new routine, the visual supports function like simple curricular modifications. A child who demonstrates aggressive behavior may need repeated ELO to learn how to share preferred materials without hitting. This type of intervention is not easy, but by spending time with the child *before* the challenging behavior occurs, teaching is more effective and the entire classroom climate is improved because the disruptive behavior is prevented.

When deciding what type of intervention to use with a child, it is helpful to systematically collect information about the child and the behavior. The problem-solving framework provides a series of steps that the team can complete in order to collect information that will lead to a potential solution for the problem (Koegel, Koegel, & Dunlap, 1996). Once you begin to use this framework to address challenging behaviors, you will realize that although many of the behaviors that occur in preschool classrooms are quickly resolved through intervention, others are not. It is important to monitor (i.e., collect data about) the child's behavior to make sure that the challenging behavior is decreasing. If not, you may need to reassess the behavior and try a different intervention.

PROBLEM-SOLVING FRAMEWORK FOR CHALLENGING BEHAVIORS

The following list outlines a system of addressing challenging behaviors in the classroom. This system includes the careful assessment, planning, and implementation of teaching plans that are used throughout the Building Blocks model. The system described here is similar to a *functional behavior assessment (FBA)* that is required by the Individuals with Disabilities Education Act (IDEA) Amendments of 1997 (PL 105-17) for children with challenging behaviors.

1. Define the challenging behavior.
2. Assess where and when the behavior is a problem.
3. Assess where and when the behavior is *not* a problem.
4. Assess what happens before and after the challenging behavior.
5. Assess classroom supports (e.g., adult, instructional, environmental).
6. Assess classroom barriers.
7. Determine what the child is attempting to communicate with the behavior.
8. Select an intervention.
9. Implement the intervention.
10. Monitor child behavior to ensure change.
11. Monitor the implementation to make sure that the adults are doing what they planned to do.

The purpose of an FBA is to determine what function the behavior is serving for the child (Davis, 1998). In other words, an FBA attempts to determine what is motivating the behavior and what the child is communicating when he or she demonstrates the behavior. If the child with whom you are working has an IFSP or an IEP and demonstrates challenging behavior, you should conduct an FBA before you begin intervention.

The representative from the school district is a key member of the team. This individual knows the district's procedures and can provide appropriate forms and assist with designing the FBA and subsequent intervention.

Grace decided that she was trying to do too many different things at once, and she felt that she was ignoring the basics of good planning and classroom arrangement. One afternoon Grace and her team decided to use the Quality Classroom Assessment and make plans for changing two or three simple things. After reviewing their current practices, Grace and her team decided to implement the following three changes:

1. They developed a regular schedule and stuck to it. They also made a copy of the schedule with pictures and taught the children how to predict what the next activity will be.

2. They provided more choices during center time and limited the number of children that can be in the center.

3. They increased the number of positive statements they made to children every day.

Making these changes was hard work at first, but Grace is so proud of the results. After only 2 weeks, the children know the routine, and everyone in the classroom seems happier and calmer. Grace is excited and has already planned another staff meeting in a month to see if more changes are necessary.

After examining the situation, Drew's team thought the best way to proceed was to use a picture schedule in the classroom and help Drew attend to the pictures and follow through at each transition. After trying this for 2 weeks with no change in behavior, the team decided to do something different. This time they decided to make Drew a series of transition cards using symbols the teacher downloaded from a web site. When it was time for a transition, the teacher simply put the appropriate symbol in Drew's hand and said, "Drew, it is time to go to circle." It worked! After only 1 week, Drew was making transitions with no problem. His teacher has made a set of these cards for home and the child care center to see if they can help with his transition problems in those settings.

Chapter 10

Emergent Literacy in the Early Childhood Classroom

Samisha's teacher helps her off the bus. Samisha holds two bear-shaped pieces of brown construction paper. She is excited to tell her teacher that she read two books last night, Big Red Barn *and* I Went Walking. *The teacher notices that Samisha's grandmother has written the title of each book on the bears, and Samisha has written her name on them. Samisha gives a "literacy bag" containing the two books back to her teacher.*

Later that day, Samisha is playing at the dramatic play area. The area is decorated as a doctor's office. Two of Samisha's classmates are sitting in child-sized chairs and looking through magazines while they wait to see the "doctor." Samisha is holding a clipboard with a piece of paper that has pictures and words for different body parts. Samisha is examining the assistant teacher who is prompting Samisha to attend to the pictures and words as she conducts the check-up. Soon, the teacher rings the bell, and after cleaning up, the children rush over to story time. These activities are all part of the teacher's plan to support the emergent literacy skills of Samisha and her classmates.

Emergent literacy is the process of becoming a reader and a writer. Children begin learning about reading and writing in the preschool years. During the preschool years, the primary milestones in developing literacy skills are oral language skills and phonological awareness, print motivation and appreciation for literate forms, and print awareness and letter knowledge (Adams, 1990; National Research Council, 1998, 1999; Neuman, Copple, & Bredekamp, 1999).

Learning to read is a complex process that requires understanding of the sound system of a written language (i.e., the phonological system) and the symbol system of that language (i.e., the alphabet). Before children can make sense of the printed symbols, they must understand that the sounds used in speech are the same sounds that are used in print. This understanding of the sound system is known as *phonological awareness.* Phonological awareness and *phonemic awareness,* the ability to recognize that a spoken word consists of a sequence of sounds, are critical skills in the acquisition of reading. Phonemic awareness is a necessary, but not sufficient, prerequisite to later growth in reading skill. Phonemic awareness and letter–sound knowledge are needed in combination to promote the acquisition of reading skills.

WHY IS EMERGENT LITERACY SO IMPORTANT FOR YOUNG CHILDREN WITH DISABILITIES?

Children with disabilities and special needs are at risk for communication and language delays. Many of the learning objectives that teachers identify in the areas of communication and language help lay the foundation for literacy. However, sometimes young children do not receive important instruction in other emergent literacy skills because of their language delays. There are important prerequisite skills in reading that every young child should learn in order to become an effective reader.

Common Concerns

Sometimes ECE teachers become concerned when the discussion turns to early or emergent literacy. Here are three common questions.

1. **Am I supposed to teach preschoolers to read?** No. It is not appropriate to teach formal reading to preschool children. However, the preschool classroom can be structured to facilitate the development of emergent literacy knowledge, which, in turn, facilitates later conventional literacy.

2. **What should a preschool teacher do to facilitate the development of emergent literacy knowledge?** The joint position statement of the National Association for the Education of Young Children (NAEYC) and the International Reading Association (IRA) states that "a central goal during these preschool years is to enhance children's exposure to and

concepts about print" (Neuman, Copple, & Bredekamp, 1999, p. 33). Preschool teachers and child care providers can use a variety of strategies to facilitate emergent literacy knowledge. This chapter is organized around the areas in which preschool teachers can facilitate emergent literacy knowledge. These areas are 1) designing literacy centers, 2) creating literacy-rich play settings, and 3) embedding literacy into specific activities. Thus, supporting emergent literacy includes both curricular modifications and ELO.

3. **What about the children with disabilities?** Children with language and other communicative delays represent a substantial portion of children eligible for special education. Although expressive language is often the high-priority goal for these children, their early education should also include the early literacy experiences described in this chapter. Our expectation is that they will be readers and writers; their preschool teachers must provide the experiences that build these literacy skills. Similarly, children with cognitive delays, sensory impairments, and other disabilities must have early experiences that excite their imaginations, promote their understanding of the meaning of print, and open doors to the potential for reading and writing. Curriculum modifications and ELOs will be matched to the child's needs and might include the use of large-print books, other adapted books, audiotapes, computer applications, and pre-braille activities.

Table 1 contains a literacy checklist for teachers to assess the literacy features of their classroom. See if you have all of the elements present in your program. If not, think about how you can implement them in your classroom.

Table 1.   Important elements for supporting emergent literacy

Comfortable places for children to sit (e.g., small couches, floor pillows)

Places for adults and children to sit together

Different types of books (e.g., noisy, alphabet, touch and feel, and rhyming books; books with repetitive phrases; books featuring children with disabilities; books featuring children of various ethnic and cultural identities)

Five books for each child in the class, rotated frequently

A listening center with tape player, headphones, and cassettes

A writing center with individual journals and many writing implements

Books made by the children in the class

A book repair box

Scheduled times for children to look at books independently and to be read to

Print that is displayed purposefully around the room (not just clutter)

Parents involved in literacy activities

Access to books children can take home with them

Meaningful conversations between adults and children throughout the day

Letter and sound games that teachers play with children (e.g., rhyming, clapping syllables of names)

DESIGNING LITERACY CENTERS

Literacy centers are specific learning environments designed to facilitate the development of emergent literacy knowledge. They provide children with opportunities to interact with print in a meaningful and purposeful way. In addition to emergent literacy knowledge about the purpose and functions of print, knowledge about the conventions of print is important. Reading is done page by page, from left to right, and top to bottom. When children engage in literacy behaviors such as pretend reading and pretend writing, they are experimenting with such conventions of print.

The literacy center is an integrated reading, writing, and listening center and should be a fun and exciting place for children to spend time. The center ought to be well stocked with a variety of culturally appropriate books, fiction and nonfiction, and attractively displayed on open shelves. The classroom library should have at least five frequently rotated books per child. A book rotation plan helps keep the book selection novel and interesting for children.

The area should be warm and inviting and provide many activities and plenty of soft places for children to settle in with a book. There should be room for a child and a friend to lay down and flip through a big book, and spaces for adults to sit down and read with a child or a small group of children. A child-sized table allows children to sit and listen to books on tapes or to write in their journals. A magnetic board on the wall with magnet letters and numbers lets children manipulate letters.

The writing area of the literacy center should have individual journals, plenty of paper, and many writing implements such as pencils, markers, crayons, and colored pencils. Encourage children to write and bind their own books with staplers. Letter and name stencils can encourage children to write their names and copy letters. A message center, where children have individual "mailboxes," may be available to encourage writing and delivering personal notes to each other.

As a part of the literacy center, the listening area includes a tape player, headphones, and several books paired with the audiocassette versions of them. If there is more than one pair of headphones, children can listen together. Young children may need to be taught how to use the audiotape player independently. Because it is difficult to find recorded books in languages other than English, parent volunteers can be asked to record stories in their home language for the children to enjoy.

CREATING LITERACY-RICH PLAY SETTINGS

Books and literacy activities should not be confined to the literacy center in the classroom. The classroom should display signs and labels that have real purposes such as the names of today's helpers, classroom attendance, message boxes, menus, and directions for washing hands. Opportunities for children to interact with print should be present throughout the classroom. For example, magazines and telephone books can be placed in the dramatic play area; in the block area, there can be books about different houses, construction, and "blueprints"; in the art area, books about color and shapes can be placed; and books can be made available on the bus. Bus drivers can play books on audiotape for children to listen to while riding to and from school.

The effects of literacy-enriched play are greater when an adult assists children in their play (Neuman & Roskos, 1993). For example, a teacher can ask a child to help read the lunch menu, help a child write a shopping list, or ask to see the "doctor's chart" in the dramatic play area. In addition, opportunities for children to write can be provided throughout the classroom. For example, in the dramatic play area, there can be message pads by the telephone, order forms at the "restaurant," and stationery and envelopes in the "post office."

Embedding Literacy in Daily Activities

Sometimes, especially for children with disabilities, encouraging emergent literacy knowledge requires the teacher to implement purposeful strategies. In the preschool classroom, emergent literacy knowledge is generally learned through participation and engagement in literacy activities and events. Some activities need to be structured to provide opportunities for emergent literacy learning, and some children do not take advantage of the learning opportunities provided in the literacy-rich play centers. Thus, strategies for specifically encouraging emergent literacy knowledge are needed. (See Chapter 6 for ELO strategies.)

Literacy-related instruction can be provided during large-group activities, free-play time, and small-group activities. Literacy activities include book reading, alphabet activities, phonemic awareness activities, and extension activities.

Reading with Children

The NAEYC/IRA position identifies reading aloud to children as the single most important activity for encouraging emergent literacy knowledge. Just reading aloud to children, however, does not provide as many opportunities for developing literacy knowledge as strategic reading aloud. Some story reading strategies that teachers can implement to encourage emergent literacy knowledge include:

- Schedule time to read aloud two or three times each day. Young children will not sit in a group for long periods of time. In a part-day program, story time should occur at least twice a day. These could be scheduled at the beginning of the morning, right before or after snack time, or before preparation to go home. Story times should occur at predictable times each day so that children know you will read to them.

- Select books with care. Many kinds of children's books are available. Along with storybooks, there are concept books, counting and number books, folk and fairy tale books, informational books, and poetry and songbooks. Varying the type of books read aloud to children helps them understand that print is used in many ways.

- Read aloud books that fit into thematic units you are teaching. Many preschool classrooms organize activities around specific themes or units. One week, the theme may be animals; the next week, weather; and another week, a holiday. It is generally easy to select some theme-related books that can be read during story time. Care should be taken to select age-appropriate books with plenty of pictures and a well-written story. Ask a librarian for recommendations.

- Read books that draw attention to the sounds of language. Probably the most natural way to encourage development of phonological awareness is by reading and re-reading books that provide opportunities for children to experiment with language sounds. These books make obvious use of rhyme, alliteration, and other phonemic manipulations that facilitate phonological awareness. ECE teachers can draw children's attention to language sounds by simply commenting on the language use, "That's funny, the way it goes *bat, boat, baby,*" or, "Did you notice that *bat, boat,* and *baby* all begin with the /b/ sound?" Children also should be encouraged to orally participate by reciting along with you when they can. The purpose is to simply draw the children's attention to the language sounds, not to take away from the language-rich experience of listening to and participating in the story reading.

- Read books that have repeating and predictable patterns of text. Many children's books have repeating lines of text that allow the children to predict the following text. For example, children learn very quickly that the pigs in *The Three Little Pigs* are going to say, "Not by the hair on my chinny, chin, chin." Many predictable books easily allow children to participate in the story reading activity.

- Let the children know that you think reading and story time are important. Making story time a predictable part of each day gives the message that you value reading and story time. You can also give the message that reading and story time are important by prominently displaying books you have recently read during story time in the literacy center. In fact, the books that children are most likely to select from the classroom literacy center are books that have recently been read aloud during story time.

- Make book introductions special. The first time you read a book to the children, be sure to introduce the book. Take a minute before reading the book to define the new words that the children will encounter. Talk about the book before reading it, and ask children to predict from the title or cover what the story will be about or what might happen. After reading, talk to the children about the story, the characters, and the events, and entertain their questions and comments. Children can help re-tell the story.

Book handling skills can also be taught. Children should be explicitly taught how to handle and care for books. Model how to hold the book, turn the pages carefully, and return the book to the shelf. Label the parts of the book before reading (e.g., "This is the front of the book, this is the back of the book, and this is the spine"). Talk about repairing books when they are accidentally torn or damaged. Creating a "book repair box" is another way to support proper book handling skills. When children notice a damaged book, they can place it in the repair box for the teacher or assistant to tape up, restaple, or clean.

Here are some basic rules of thumb when reading to a group of children:

- Read with expression
- Hold the book so the children can see it
- Point out objects in the pictures, and allow the children to do so, too
- Sometimes follow the words with your fingers (so that children begin to understand reading goes from left to right and from top to bottom)

Alphabet and Phonemic Awareness Activities

Knowing the alphabet is one of the strongest predictors of short- and long-term literacy success (Stevenson & Newman, 1986). One reason that letter name knowledge is valuable is that 18 letters closely map onto one specific sound or phoneme, like the letters *b, d,* or *p.* So, knowing letter names helps speed up the acquisition of some phonological sensitivity skills and understanding of letter–sound relationships (Stahl & Murray, 1994). Furthermore, being able to recognize letters quickly and accurately is a necessary prerequisite for later reading.

Reading alphabet books with examples of words illustrating various phonemic sounds can increase children's knowledge of the alphabet and help children achieve higher levels of phonological awareness (Murray, Stahl, & Ivey, 1996). Games such as Lotto or Concentration, which require children to identify letters, are another useful activity. Alphabets should be placed where young children can see, touch, and manipulate the letters and use them where they work and play.

Phonemic awareness activities should happen daily. Activities that help facilitate phonological and phonemic awareness include rhyming, reading alliterative books, grouping objects that begin with the same sound, syllable-focused songs and games, and "say it and move it" activities (e.g., Blachman, Ball, Black, & Tangel, 2000). For example, the teacher might excuse the children from circle time by saying a word

Table 2. Tips for teaching emergent literacy skills

Child-focused instructional strategies (CFIS)	Systematically teach a child to look at a book using prompting and reinforcement techniques
	Teach a child who is making the transition to kindergarten to write his or her name using direct instruction and graduated guidance
	Use time delays to increase commenting when a child is looking at a preferred book
	Address matching skills by using examples of environmental print and discrete trial teaching techniques
	Teach a child to answer questions about a story by using visual support strategies and systematically fade those prompts
Embedded learning opportunities (ELO)	Address holding a writing utensil through a preferred activity such as signing up to use the computer
	Address language comprehension (an important prerequisite to reading comprehension) through reading stories and asking questions about preferred topics
	Teach awareness of environmental print through art projects, including collages from magazines and newspaper circulars
	Target letter sounds by using alphabet blocks in the construction area
	Use sound lotto games to enhance listening skills
	Use a Scrabble board to enhance matching skills and patterning skills
Curriculum modifications (CM)	Use books about highly preferred topics
	Use modified writing materials (e.g., foam grips on pens)
	Use modified writing surfaces (e.g., slant boards and tabletop easels)
	Include writing materials in many different centers (e.g., dramatic play to take orders at the restaurant, science center to write down observations, manipulatives to trace block patterns)
	Increase name recognition by requiring children to "sign up" for highly preferred centers and jobs using name tags
High-quality early childhood environment	Construct literacy-rich centers including, but not limited to, a library center, a writing center, and literacy and writing props in dramatic play
	Create a print-rich classroom
	Schedule regular story times
	Conduct phonological awareness activities including rhyming and sound awareness

that rhymes with their name. "Whose name sounds like melon? Right! It is Helen."

SUMMARY

This chapter describes early literacy milestones, summarizes research-based activities, and introduces a strategy for implementing a literacy-infused environment. Reading is a complex and multifaceted process, and children need an approach to learning that integrates many elements and that begins early in their lives. ECE and ECSE teachers have the opportunity and the obligation to help children develop skills required for learning to read. Using a literacy-infused approach with well-integrated, meaningful literacy experiences for young children will build a solid foundation of language and literacy skills for future success.

Friendships and Social Relationships

Nhan is interested in his peers but is not very successful in initiating interactions with them. No one seems to mind having him around, but he has not formed any friendships. His teachers are concerned that he is beginning to spend more and more time in solitary play activities, but they're not sure what to do.

Mr. Alvarez is a first-year teacher in an inclusive ECE program. During his master's degree program, he was always very interested in the classes about social development. He had planned to implement state-of-the-art social interaction strategies in his classroom, but so far he is overwhelmed with the day-to-day logistics of running the classroom. What can he do to implement these strategies in his classroom?

Discussions of young children's social relationships involve three main concepts to consider: *friendships, social acceptance,* and *social rejection.* These terms are not discrete terms but rather points along a continuum of relationships that occur in an inclusive classroom.

Two children are *friends* when they choose to play with each other more than with other children. These children often seek each other out to sit beside in class or to walk with during transitions. True friendships are reciprocal: Both children identify each other as friends and are equally likely to initiate interactions. *Social acceptance* means that other children in the class play with the child; they smile at the child and are happy to sit beside him or her at snack time. Whereas friendship is an active relationship, social acceptance is more passive. Some children in preschool classrooms are *socially rejected.* Peers in the class may not choose the child to play with, they may ask the child to leave a play activity, and they may refuse the child's requests to join an activity. Children who are socially rejected by some peers usually do not have any friends.

Developing positive peer relationships is a major developmental accomplishment of early childhood. In the context of peer relationships, children develop important communication, social, play, and cognitive skills. Playful social interactions with peers are an essential part of the early childhood years. Children who make friends during preschool often have better social and academic outcomes. Children who are socially rejected tend to have poorer mental health and academic outcomes. (To read more about friendships, see Meyer, Park, Grenot-Scheyer, Schwartz, & Harry, 1998).

WHAT SKILLS ARE INVOLVED IN FORMING FRIENDSHIPS AND SOCIAL RELATIONSHIPS?

In order for children to develop friendships, children need to have many opportunities to interact successfully. These interactions can be simple (e.g., passing materials at the snack table) or more complex and extended (e.g., working together on a cooperative art project). Teachers play an important role in planning and supporting these activities. Instruction to develop social relationships should occur every day and across all classroom areas and activities. The teacher's role in supporting positive social relationships is often a delicate balance between helping and stepping back. The teacher should facilitate children's interaction but not interfere or take over the situation.

Teachers can not only arrange their classroom environments to support positive social interactions, but they can also teach their students skills that are key to positive relationships. These skills include, but are not limited to

- Being aware of others
- Sharing
- Helping others
- Persisting or making efforts to maintain social interactions

- Organizing play with others
- Being able to enter play situations
- Negotiating
- Solving conflicts

As with all skills, friendship skills can be incorporated into the general curriculum, and teachers should identify friendship learning objectives for children who are struggling with interaction.

Strategies To Promote Friendships and Social Relationships

The teacher or the team may use the steps outlined in Chapter 4 to identify learning objectives, to plan the level of intervention, to determine when and where to intervene, and to evaluate the effects of their intervention. As always, teams need to select the appropriate level of support, whether it's a curriculum modification, an ELO, or more explicit instruction, such as CFIS.

When making plans to support social relationships, one of the most important features is to make sure that the classroom provides social opportunities. Some ways to do this include selecting activities and materials that require more than one child to participate. Some materials are more social than others (e.g., playing ball games, dramatic play), but even seemingly solitary activities (e.g., puzzles, computer games) can be arranged to require a social component. Another point to remember is that if the aim is to teach social skills, the team should try to incorporate this teaching and learning within activities that build on children's interests and experiences.

Planned classroom activities can also incorporate social opportunities. For example, pairs or small groups of children can make murals, build sculptures, or write storybooks. Sometimes children who lack social skills have difficulty with more open-ended activities. The teacher can provide structure by using visual supports. In the dramatic play area, for example, a photo display can provide children with a "script" to get them started.

Routine classroom activities can also be used to promote social relationships. One simple way to do this is to change the lines of children's songs, rhymes, or games to insert a social term or encourage interaction. These are called *group friendship activities* (Cooper & McEvoy, 1996). An example from the Hokey Pokey would be to change one of the lines to something like, "you shake your neighbor's hand."

Children need extended and repeated interactions with peers in order to develop friendships and social relationships that extend beyond the immediate teaching situation. Part of the team's planning involves assuring repeated and successful social interactions in the classroom and on the playground. Odom and colleagues (1999) offered additional advice for supporting social relationships and developing friendships. Young children also meet potential friends in their neighborhoods and communities. Hanson and Beckman (2001) described strategies that parents can use to help their children make friends.

Nhan's team took another look at his current performance in the classroom and decided to do two things. First, when planning his special language instruction sessions, whether using ELO or CFIS, the team decided to have peers participate in the session or learning opportunity. Second, they planned more social opportunities for him by seating him next to preferred peers at snack time and circle time and by adding a preferred social activity during their outdoor time. They've already noticed that Nhan is spending more time with some of his pals.

Table 1.   Tips for facilitating friendships and social relationships

Child-focused instruction strategies (CFIS)	Systematically teach children to take turns with peers within a highly preferred activity
	Teach children who are developing typically to initiate to and be persistent with children with disabilities
	Teach children with disabilities to compliment a child before attempting to join an ongoing activity
	Using direct-instruction methods, teach children with disabilities to answer questions during play activities
	Teach specific play routines that include peers such as playing with dolls or playing with cars and trucks
Embedded learning opportunities (ELO)	Plan dramatic play activities with specific roles (e.g., grocer, shopper, shelf stocker) and assign the roles
	Include group friendship activities, such as exchanging hugs and "high-fives" during songs, group meetings, or other planned activities
	Sabotage a small-group art activity by giving insufficient materials; encourage the children to problem solve how to share and take turns
	Set up a "PALS" center during free-choice time; children play with special toys and games that require working as a dyad
	Assign two children at a time to complete classroom jobs
Curriculum modifications (CM)	Select and have available materials and equipment that facilitate social interaction (e.g., wagon, puppets, board games)
	Carefully select the members of small groups in order to facilitate social interaction
	Use visual supports to help children solve conflicts
	Make transition times social times by pairing children
	Have children share or pass materials at circle time and snack time
High-quality early childhood environment	Provide opportunities to observe and interact with socially competent peers
	Plan cooperative activities that require more than one child
	Use classroom environments that encourage two or more children working together on projects and activities
	Provide both structured and unstructured play times
	Read books and have class discussions about friendship, problem solving, and conflict resolution

Mr. Alvarez decided to implement group friendship activities in his classroom. Every day at circle time, he has one activity in which children shake hands, give "high fives," or pass a toy around the circle. After he implemented these group friendship activities, he observed that more children were playing together at free-choice time, and no one was being rejected anymore. He was pleased by these results and impressed with how easy it was to implement this strategy.

Table 1 provides some additional ideas for facilitating friendships and social relationships using the Building Blocks framework.

Chapter 12

Concluding Thoughts

Inclusion is about belonging and participating in a diverse society. Inclusion of young children with disabilities and other special needs in early childhood classrooms is now a primary service option supported by research. A substantial number of research studies report positive outcomes for children with disabilities and children without disabilities in inclusive settings (Odom, 2000). Research also identifies some of the challenges and complexities of inclusion. One of the challenges is how to provide the specialized instruction needed by children with special needs without interfering with the social ecology or curricular integrity of the inclusive classroom.

The Building Blocks model offers practical suggestions to help teachers accomplish this task. This book offers teachers in early childhood classrooms practical strategies for including and teaching young children with special needs. Our aim is to help teachers make good decisions when selecting and using appropriate levels of assistance, working in teams, and using effective teaching strategies to help children attain important and worthwhile objectives.

Specialized instruction is an important component of inclusion. It is the cornerstone of special education. That is, a stated aim of education is to enhance young children's development and learning by teaching new skills, by attempting to remediate delays, and by preventing secondary disabilities. Yet, in our efforts to enhance children's development and learning, we must remember that the early childhood curriculum is broad and that there are many important things for young children to learn during the preschool years. For example, children expand their communication skills and begin learn about reading and writing. They learn to get along with others and make friends. They refine their physical abilities. They learn to solve problems. Always, we want to promote a positive attitude toward learning and life. Thus, our teaching efforts in inclusive classrooms must focus on the whole child and appreciate all of these important areas of learning.

Inclusion is not simply about the social experience. One of the repeated findings of the inclusion research is that just "being there" is not sufficient. There are critical features that are necessary for any child's early learning experiences. Their development must be nurtured. Their experiences must be developmentally appropriate and individually planned. The child must be supported so that he or she may take advantage of the full complement of learning experiences.

The Building Blocks model recognizes that providing individualized, specialized instruction in busy, action-packed classrooms is difficult. The model provides teachers with a range of supports and instruction that is necessary to make inclusion successful. It takes planning and attention. And, it is rewarding. Successful teaching results in children learning the valuable skills and behaviors we have identified for them and being able to use them in meaningful ways. Successful teaching means that children will learn and thrive in your classroom.

References

Adams, M.J. (1990). *Beginning to read: Thinking and learning about print.* Cambridge, MA: The MIT Press.

Allen, K.E., & Schwartz, I.S. (2001). *The exceptional child: Inclusion in early childhood education.* Albany, NY: Delmar.

Azrin, N., & Foxx, R. (1989). *Toilet training in less than a day.* New York: Pocket Books.

Baker, B.L., & Brightman, A.J. (with Blacher, J.B., Heifetz, L.J., Hinshaw, S.P., & Murphy, D.M.). (1997). *Steps to independence: Teaching everyday skills to children with special needs* (3rd ed.). Baltimore: Paul H. Brookes Publishing Co.

Blachman, B.A., Ball, E.W., Black, R., & Tangel, D.M. (2000). *Road to the code: A phonological awareness program for young children.* Baltimore: Paul H. Brookes Publishing Co.

Bredekamp, S., & Copple, C. (1997). *Developmentally appropriate practice in early childhood programs.* Washington, DC: National Association for the Education of Young Children (NAEYC).

Bricker, D. (with Pretti-Frontczak, K., & McComas, N.). (1998). *An activity-based approach to early intervention* (2nd ed.). Baltimore: Paul H. Brookes Publishing Co.

Bricker, D., & Waddell, M. (2002). *Assessment, Evaluation, and Programming System (AEPS): Vol. 4. AEPS curriculum for three to six years.* (2nd ed.). Baltimore: Paul H. Brookes Publishing Co.

Cooper, C.S., & McEvoy, M.A. (1996). Group friendship activities: An easy way to develop the social skills of young children. *Teaching Exceptional Children, 28*(3), 67–69.

Davis, C. (1998). Functional assessment: Issues in implementation and applied research. *Preventing School Failure, 43,* 34–36.

Davis, M.D., Kilgo, J.L., & Gamel-McCormick, M. (1998). *Young children with special needs: A developmentally appropriate approach.* Needham Heights, MA: Allyn & Bacon.

Dodge, D., & Colker, L. (1992). *The creative curriculum for early childhood* (3rd ed.). Washington, DC: Teaching Strategies.

Filler, J. (1996). A comment on inclusion: Research and social policy. *Society for Research in Child Development Policy Report, 10*(2–3), 31–34.

Friend, M., & Cook, L. (2000). *Interactions: Collaboration skills for school professionals* (3rd ed.). White Plains, NY: Longman.

Giangreco, M., Dennis, R., Edelman, S., & Cloninger, C. (1994). Dressing your IEPs for the general education climate: Analysis of IEP goals and objectives for students with multiple disabilities. *Remedial and Special Education, 15,* 288–326.

Hanson, M.J., & Beckman, P.J. (2001). *Me, too!* (Vols. 1–6). Baltimore: Paul H. Brookes Publishing Co.

Harms, T., Clifford, R., & Cryer, D. (1998). *Early childhood environment rating scale* (Rev. ed.). New York: Teachers College Press.

Hohmann, M., & Weikart, D. (1995). *Educating young children: Active learning practices for preschool and child care programs.* Ypsilanti, MI: High/Scope Press.

Hunter, D., Bailey, A., & Taylor, B. (1995). *Zen of groups: A handbook for people meeting with a purpose.* Tucson, AZ: Fisher Books.

Koegel, L.K., Koegel, R.L., & Dunlap, G. (Eds.). (1996). *Positive behavioral support: Including people with difficult behavior in the community.* Baltimore: Paul H. Brookes Publishing Co.

McCormick, L., & Feeney, S. (1995). Modifying and expanding activities for children with disabilities. *Young Children, 50*(4), 10–17.

Melloy, K., Davis, C., Wehby, J., Murry, F., & Leiber, J. (1998). *Developing social competence in children and youth with challenging behaviors: From the Second CCBD Mini-Library Series. Successful interventions for the 21st century.* Reston, VA: Council for Children with Behavioral Disorders.

Meyer, L.H., Park, H.S., Grenot-Scheyer, M., Schwartz, I.S., & Harry, B. (Eds.). (1998). *Making friends: The influences of culture and development.* Baltimore: Paul H. Brookes Publishing Co.

Murray, B.A., Stahl, S.A., & Ivey, M.G. (1996). Developing phoneme awareness through alphabet books. *Reading and Writing, 8,* 307–322.

National Research Council. (1998). *Preventing reading difficulties in young children.* Washington, DC: National Academy Press.

National Research Council. (1999). *Starting out right: A guide to promoting children's research success.* Washington, DC: National Academy Press.

Neuman, S.B., Copple, C., & Bredekamp, S. (1999). *Learning to read and write: Developmentally appropriate practices for young children.* Washington, DC: National Association for the Education of Young Children (NAEYC).

Neuman, S.B., & Roskos, K. (1993). Access to print for children of poverty: Differential effects of adult mediation and literacy-enriched play settings on environmental and functional print tasks. *American Educational Research Journal, 30,* 95–122.

Odom, S.L. (2000). Preschool inclusion: What we know and where we go from here. *Topics in Early Childhood Special Education, 20*(1), 20–27.

Odom, S.L., Horn, E.M., Marquart, J.M., Hanson, M.J., Wolfberg, P., Beckman, P., Lieber, J., Li, S., Schwartz, I., Janko, S., & Sandall, S. (1999). On the forms of inclusion: Organizational context and individualized service models. *Journal of Early Intervention, 22,* 185–199.

Odom, S.L., McConnell, S., McEvoy, M., Peterson, C., Ostrosky, M., Chandler, L., Spicuzza, R., Skellenger, A., Creighton, M., & Favazza, P. (1999). Relative effects of interventions supporting the social competence of young children with disabilities. *Topics in Early Childhood Special Education, 19,* 75–91.

Odom, S.L., Peck, C.A., Hanson, M.J., Beckman, P.J., Kaiser, A.P., Lieber, J., Brown, W.H., Horn, E.M., & Schwartz, I.S. (1996). Inclusion at the preschool level: An ecological systems analysis. *Society for Research in Child Development Policy Report, 10,* 18–30.

Pugach, M.C., & Johnson, L.J. (1995). *Collaborative practitioners, collaborative schools.* Denver, CO: Love Publishing.

Sandall, S., & Ostrosky, M. (Eds.). (1999). Practical ideas for addressing challenging behaviors. *Young Exceptional Children Monograph Series, 1.*

Stahl, S.A., & Murray, B.A. (1994). Defining phonological awareness and its relationship to early reading. *Journal of Educational Psychology, 86,* 221–234.

Stevenson, H.W., & Newman, R.S. (1986). Long-term prediction of achievement and attitudes in mathematics and reading. *Child Development, 57,* 646–659.

Villa, R.A., & Thousand, J.S. (1992). Student collaboration: An essential for curriculum delivery in the 21st century. In S. Stainback & W. Stainback (Eds.), *Curriculum considerations in inclusive classrooms: Facilitating learning for all students* (pp. 117–142). Baltimore: Paul H. Brookes Publishing Co.

Wolery, M., & Wilbers, J.S. (1994). *Including children with special needs in early childhood programs.* Washington, DC: National Association for the Education of Young Children.

Appendix A

Blank Forms

The Team Agenda

Date: _____

Team members: _____   _____

_____   _____

_____   _____

Facilitator: _____

Recorder: _____

Timekeeper: _____

Agenda item	Time

Problem-Solving Worksheet

Date: _____

Team members: _____ _____

_____ _____

_____ _____

Problem: _____

Solution to be tried: _____

What is the task?	Who will do it?	By when?

Outcomes: _____

_____

_____

_____

Quality Classroom Assessment Form

Date: _____

Classroom: _____

Team members: _____   _____

_____   _____

Goal: _____

Indicator	Yes	No	Not sure	Examples
1. Do children spend most of their time playing and working with materials or with other children?				
2. Do children have access to various activities throughout the day?				
3. Do teachers work with individual children, small groups, and the whole group at different times during the day?				
4. Is the classroom decorated with children's original artwork, their own writing, and stories they've dictated?				
5. Do children learn within meaningful (i.e., relevant to their interests and experiences) contexts?				

Building Blocks for Teaching Preschoolers with Special Needs by Susan R. Sandall and Ilene S. Schwartz with Gail E. Joseph, Hsin-Ying Chou, Eva M. Horn, Joan Lieber, Samuel L. Odom, and Ruth Wolery   © 2002 by Paul H. Brookes Publishing Co.

(continued)

Quality Classroom Assessment Form

(continued)

Indicator	Yes	No	Not sure	Examples
6. Do children work on projects and have periods of time to play and explore?				
7. Do children have an opportunity to play and explore?				
8. Do teachers read books to children individually or in small groups throughout the day?				
9. Is the curriculum adapted for those who are ahead as well as those who need additional help?				
10. Do the children and their families feel safe and secure within their early childhood program?				

Notes: _____

_____

_____

_____

Building Blocks for Teaching Preschoolers with Special Needs by Susan R. Sandall, and Ilene S. Schwartz with Gail E. Joseph, Hsin-Ying Chou, Eva M. Horn, Joan Lieber, Samuel L. Odom, and Ruth Wolery   © 2002 by Paul H. Brookes Publishing Co.

Classroom Action Worksheet

Date: _____

Team members: _____

Indicator	What's the problem?	What can we do?	Who will do it?	By when?

Building Blocks for Teaching Preschoolers with Special Needs by Susan R. Sandall and Ilene S. Schwartz
with Gail E. Joseph, Hsin-Ying Chou, Eva M. Horn, Joan Lieber, Samuel L. Odom, and Ruth Wolery   © 2002 by Paul H. Brookes Publishing Co.

Child Assessment Worksheet

Teacher's name: _____

Date: _____

Child's name: _____

Classroom activities	Classroom expectations	Child's level of performance
		Strength ____ Average ____ Area of concern ____
		Strength ____ Average ____ Area of concern ____
		Strength ____ Average ____ Area of concern ____
		Strength ____ Average ____ Area of concern ____

Building Blocks for Teaching Preschoolers with Special Needs by Susan R. Sandall and Ilene S. Schwartz
with Gail E. Joseph, Hsin-Ying Chou, Eva M. Horn, Joan Lieber, Samuel L. Odom, and Ruth Wolery   © 2002 by Paul H. Brookes Publishing Co.

Planning Worksheet

Teacher's name: _____

Child's name: _____

This planning guide will help you collect more specific information for areas of concern for specific children. Using the *Child Assessment Worksheet*, identify three activities on which you would like to focus your attention. Once you identify the problem, collecting information is the next step for instructional planning for children in inclusive settings.

(Key: CM = curriculum modification; ELO = embedded learning opportunity; CFIS = child-focused instructional strategies)

Activities	Define concern	What are you currently doing?	Ideas for instruction
			CM _____ ELO _____ CFIS _____ Describe:
			CM _____ ELO _____ CFIS _____ Describe:
			CM _____ ELO _____ CFIS _____ Describe:

Building Blocks for Teaching Preschoolers with Special Needs by Susan R. Sandall and Ilene S. Schwartz
with Gail E. Joseph, Hsin-Ying Chou, Eva M. Horn, Joan Lieber, Samuel L. Odom, and Ruth Wolery   © 2002 by Paul H. Brookes Publishing Co.

Child Activity Matrix

Teacher's name: _____

Date: _____   Child's name: _____

Key: CM = curriculum modification; ELO = embedded learning opportunity; CFIS = child-focused instructional strategy

Building Blocks for Teaching Preschoolers with Special Needs by Susan R. Sandall and Ilene S. Schwartz
with Gail E. Joseph, Hsin-Ying Chou, Eva M. Horn, Joan Lieber, Samuel L. Odom, and Ruth Wolery   © 2002 by Paul H. Brookes Publishing Co.

Classroom Activity Matrix

Date: _____

Teacher's name: _____

Key: CM = curriculum modification; ELO = embedded learning opportunity; CFIS = child-focused instructional strategy

Building Blocks for Teaching Preschoolers with Special Needs by Susan R. Sandall and Ilene S. Schwartz
with Gail E. Joseph, Hsin-Ying Chou, Eva M. Horn, Joan Lieber, Samuel L. Odom, and Ruth Wolery   © 2002 by Paul H. Brookes Publishing Co.

Evaluation Worksheet

Teacher's name: _____

Date: _____

Child's name: _____

Concern	Plan	Evaluation information
		Counts _____ Notes _____ Products _____ Did the plan work? Yes _____ No What will you do next week?
		Counts _____ Notes _____ Products _____ Did the plan work? Yes _____ No What will you do next week?
		Counts _____ Notes _____ Products _____ Did the plan work? Yes _____ No What will you do next week?

Building Blocks for Teaching Preschoolers with Special Needs by Susan R. Sandall and Ilene S. Schwartz
with Gail E. Joseph, Hsin-Ying Chou, Eva M. Horn, Joan Lieber, Samuel L. Odom, and Ruth Wolery   © 2002 by Paul H. Brookes Publishing Co.

ELO-at-a-Glance for: _____

Date: _____

Team members: _____   _____

_____   _____

Routine: _____

Objectives: _____

_____

What are you going to do?

What are you going to say?

How will you respond?

What materials will you need?

How many opportunities will you provide each day?

Monday	Tuesday	Wednesday	Thursday	Friday

Appendix B

Additional Readings

GENERAL EARLY CHILDHOOD EDUCATION

Bredekamp, S., & Copple, C. (1997). *Appropriate practice in early childhood programs* (Rev. ed.). Washington DC: National Association for the Education of Young Children.

Decker, C.A., & Decker, J.R. (2001). *Planning and administering early childhood programs*. Columbus, OH: Merrill.

Gordon, A., & Williams-Browne, K. (1995). *Beginnings and beyond*. Albany, NY: Delmar.

Harms, T., Clifford, R.M., & Cryer, D. (1998). *Early Childhood Rating Scale* (Rev. ed.). New York: Teachers College Press.

Harms, T., Cryer, D., & Clifford, R.M. (1990). *Infant/toddler environment rating scale*. New York: Teachers College Press.

Sandall, S.R., McLean, M.E., & Smith, B.J. (2000). *DEC recommended practices in early intervention/early childhood special education*. Longmont, CO: Sopris West.

INCLUSION

Allen, K.E., & Schwartz, I.S. (2001). *The exceptional child: Inclusion in early childhood education*. Albany, NY: Delmar.

Guralnick, M.J. (Ed.). (2001). *Early childhood inclusion: Focus on change*. Baltimore: Paul H. Brookes Publishing Co.

Peck, C.A., Odom, S.L., & Bricker, D.D. (1993). *Integrating young children with disabilities into community programs: Ecological perspectives on research and implementation*. Baltimore: Paul H. Brookes Publishing Co.

Schnorr, R.F. (1990). "Peter? He comes and goes....": First graders' perspectives on a part-time mainstream student. *The Journal of The Association for the Persons with Severe Handicaps, 15*, 231–240.

CHALLENGING BEHAVIOR

Janney, R., & Snell, M.E. (2000). *Teachers' guides to inclusive practices: Behavioral support.* Baltimore: Paul H. Brookes Publishing Co.

Jenson, W.R., Rhode, G., & Reavis, H.K. (1994). *The tough kid toolbox.* Longmont, CO: Sopris West.

Koegel, L.K., Koegel, R.L., & Dunlap, G. (Eds.). (1996). *Positive behavioral support: Including people with difficult behavior in the community.* Baltimore: Paul H. Brookes Publishing Co.

Sandall, S.R., & Ostrosky, M. (Eds.) (1999). *Practical ideas for addressing challenging behaviors.* Longmont, CO: Sopris West.

Strain, P.S., & Hemmeter, M.L. (1997). Keys to being successful when confronted with challenging behaviors. *Young Exceptional Children, 1*(1), 2–8.

CURRICULUM MODIFICATIONS

Breath, D., DeMauro, G.J., & Snyder, P. (1997). Adaptive sitting for young children with mild to moderate motor challenges: Basic guidelines. *Young Exceptional Children, 1*(1), 10–16.

Cook, R.E., Tessier, A., & Klein, M.D. (2000). *Adapting early childhood curricula for children in inclusive settings.* Columbus, OH: Merrill.

INSTRUCTIONAL STRATEGIES

Bailey, D.B., & Wolery, M. (1992). *Teaching infants and preschoolers with disabilities.* New York: Merrill.

Bricker, D., (with Pretti-Frontczak, K., & McComas, N.) (1998). *An activity-based approach to early intervention* (2nd ed.). Baltimore: Paul H. Brookes Publishing Co.

Wolery, M., & Wilbers, J.S. (Eds.) (1994). *Including children with special needs in early childhood programs.* Washington, DC: National Association for the Education of Young Children.

Woods Cripe, J., & Venn, M.L. (1997). Family guided routines for early intervention services. *Young Exceptional Children, 1*(1), 18–26.

INDEPENDENCE

Baker, B.L., & Brightman, A.J., (with Blacher, J.B., Heifetz, L.J., Hinshaw, S.P., & Murphy, D.M.) (1997). *Steps to independence: Teaching everyday skills to children with special needs* (3rd ed.). Baltimore: Paul H. Brookes Publishing Co.

Colvin, G., & Lazar, M. (1997). *The effective elementary classroom.* Longmont, CO: Sopris West.

Durand, V.M. (1998). *Sleep better! A guide to improving sleep for children with special needs.* Baltimore: Paul H. Brookes Publishing Co.

Hodgdon, L.A. (1997). *Visual strategies for improving communication.* Troy: MI: Quirk Roberts.

CLASSROOM-BASED ASSESSMENT

Cohen, D.H., Stern, V., & Balaban, N. (1994) . *Observing and recording the behavior of young children.* New York: Teachers College Press.

Cohen, L.G., & Spenciner, L.J. (1998). *Assessment of children and youth.* New York: Longman.

Losardo, A., & Notari-Syverson, A. (2001). *Alternative approaches to assessing young children.* Baltimore: Paul H. Brookes Publishing Co.

Meisels, S. (1993). Remaking classroom assessment with the Work Sampling System. *Young Children, 48*(5), 34–40.

Shores, E.F., & Grace, C. (1998). *The portfolio book: A step-by-step guide for teachers.* Beltsville, MD: Gryphon House.

LANGUAGE AND COMMUNICATION

Hart, B., & Risley, T.R. (1995). *Meaningful differences in the everyday experience of young American children.* Baltimore: Paul H. Brookes Publishing Co.

Hemmeter, M.L., & Kaiser, A.P. (1990). Environmental influences on children's language: a model and case study. *Education and Treatment of Children, 13,* 331–341.

Watson, L., Crais, E., & Layton, T. (1999). *Handbook of early language impairment in children: Assessment and intervention.* San Diego: Singular Publishing Group.

FRIENDSHIPS AND SOCIAL COMPETENCE

Hundert, J. (1995). *Enhancing social competence in young students.* Austin, TX: PRO-ED.

Paley, V. (1993). *You can't say you can't play.* Cambridge, MA: Harvard University Press.

Quill, K.A. (2000). *Do-watch-listen-say: Social and communication intervention for children with autism.* Baltimore: Paul H. Brookes Publishing Co.

Snell, M.E., & Janney, R. (2000). *Teachers' guides to inclusive practices: Social relationships and peer support.* Baltimore: Paul H. Brookes Publishing Co.

LITERACY

Adams, M. (1990). *Learning to read: Thinking and learning about print.* Cambridge, MA: MIT Press.

Adams, M.J., Foorman, B.R., Lundberg, I., & Beeler, T. (1998). *Phonemic awareness in young children: A classroom curriculum.* Baltimore: Paul H. Brookes Publishing Co.

Neuman, S., Copple, C., & Bredekamp, S. (2000). *Learning to read and write: Developmentally appropriate practices for young children.* Washington, DC: National Association for the Education of Young Children.

Neuman, S., & Roskos, K. (1993). *Language and literacy learning in the early years: An integrated approach.* San Diego: Harcourt Brace Jovanovich.

Index

Page numbers followed by *f* indicate figures; those followed by *t* indicate tables.